Traction Engine
ALBUM

Traction Engine
ALBUM

Malcolm Ranieri

THE CROWOOD PRESS

First published in 2005 by
The Crowood Press Ltd
Ramsbury, Marlborough
Wiltshire SN8 2HR

www.crowood.com

British Library Cataloguing-in-Publication Data
A catalogue record for this book is available from the British Library.

ISBN 1 86126 794 0

Note
The traction engine is graded in size by the nhp (nominal horsepower) scale, not to be
confused with hp (horsepower). This rating dates back to the very early days and was an
attempt to simplify matters for agricultural users. It is about a seventh of the power
classification of horsepower, and it is thought to have been brought in to emphasize the fact
that the machine was not formidable or frightening – an early case of spin!

Frontispiece: A 1931 Burrell road locomotive, seen on a road run in July 2004 in connection
with the Great Bucks Steam Working at Ickford.

Black and white archive photography courtesy of Mortons Heritage Media.

Typeset by Jean Cussons Typesetting, Diss, Norfolk

Printed and bound in Singapore by Craft Print International Ltd.

Contents

Foreword

'A PICTURE paints a thousand words.' This book represents many thousands of words for it is full of crisp, sharp pictures of traction engines, at work or at rest and always in a sympathetic background.

Malcolm Ranieri is a well-known figure around the traction engine preservation world. Many of us in the movement have, along with our engines, been subject to his enquiring lens; now everyone can take pleasure in the skill and ingenuity that Malcolm displays with his trusty Mamiya camera.

The world of the steam engine is fascinating for so many; it may be regarded as a disease, as once afflicted there is no cure. There are so many aspects to it: the character of the particular engine, the life it takes as it comes into steam, the people associated with the engines, and so on. This book explores all this and covers all makes that have survived into preservation along with a short history of the manufacturers.

This book contains all types of pictures from classic portraits to the full-blooded action shots. All are of the highest quality as one would expect from a man who has achieved considerable recognition in the world of photography, for Malcolm is a Fellow of the Royal Photographic Society and a Master Photographer of the Photographic Alliance of Great Britain.

This is the type of book which you can read and study for hours, or you can simply open a page and enjoy for a few moments the detail and beauty of some of Britain's finest industrial heritage.

Andrew Semple
Chairman, National Traction Engine Trust

RIGHT: *The 1918 4nhp Garrett showman's tractor 'Margaret' is seen in sparkling condition next to the gallopers at the Gloucestershire Warwickshire Railway Steam Rally in October 2002.*

OPPOSITE: *This is an interesting picture in that the 5nhp 1914 Clayton & Shuttleworth convertible traction engine is pictured in front of Shuttleworth House, where one of the firm's founders lived. This engine is part of the Shuttleworth Collection at Old Warden Aerodrome and is seen at the Bedfordshire Rally in September 2003.*

Introduction

MENTION 'steam power' and most people will think of the railway age that coincided with the birth and development of steam and which carried on well into the modern era, until the last steam locomotives were withdrawn. Steam power had many uses from its inception in the 1800s, through the Victorian age – its most glorious period – and into the 1900s and beyond. Even in the first years of this century steam has its champions, especially in preservation.

From the early 1800s inventors and promoters strove to harness this new source of power. While railways can be said to have been the most glamorous and far-reaching aspect of steam power, there were also stationary engines such as the great beam engines used in mines and industry. Steam power started to replace wind-, water-, man- and horsepower in agriculture, on the canals, rivers and seas, and in road transportation. At its height steam power touched on the lives of everybody and everything; hardly anywhere on land and water did not see some form of steam in transport or industry, and one of its major applications was in the field of road steam or traction engines.

'Traction engine' is a widely used generic term, covering portables, agricultural use, wagons and cars, road rollers, showman's engines, ploughing engines, tractors and road locomotives. Portables worked away quietly in agricultural and industrial use, belted to various equipment, sometimes fixed to frames or with free-running wheels so that they could be moved from place to place, and were the precursors of the traction engine. Agricultural engines, as the term implies, were used for farming work, especially belted to threshing machines or other equipment such as woodcutters or stone breakers. Wagons had a short life on the roads due to the rise of the diesel engine, but some manufacturers – especially Foden and Sentinel – flew the

flag for steam power up to the 1960s. Steam cars had their heyday in the first twenty-five years of the twentieth century, makes such as Stanley from America offering good performance before the internal combustion engine won the day. Road rollers are perhaps the best-known thanks to the once-everyday scene of the steam roller simmering away at the road-building site, ready to roll the new surface flat – to this day most people still refer to modern diesel rollers as 'steam rollers', so ingrained in the public mind is this form of traction engine. Showman's engines are the 'peacocks' and 'glamour' machines of the traction engine world: these goliaths moved fairground equipment around the country and became mobile generators for lighting fairgrounds at night. The mighty ploughing engines worked on farms, ploughing and drainage work being their forte, working in pairs, or in the early days using a round-robin system with one engine. Tractors and road locomotives moved various loads around the country, and in the case of the smaller tractor may have been a local small-load mover, especially useful in the timber industry.

The story of the rise of steam has often been told, but is worth repeating to set the scene. The steam engine's basic principles did not change from its inception to its demise. In very basic terms, steam is produced in a round water boiler, usually coal-fired, and passed into a cylinder that contains a piston; the steam drives the piston forward and backwards under compression, and this motion is converted via a crank to make the wheels rotate.

The principles of steam power had been known from the late middle ages (and some commentators refer back to the Greeks), but not until the late eighteenth century was it first used: strangely enough, considering all its later use in providing motive power, its first application was in pumping water out of mine shafts. 'Beam engines' were first used in British mines at the end of the eighteenth century; they were so called because a beam formed the overhead device, to which rods were attached for pumping water, powered by an open steam engine. Thomas

OPPOSITE: A 1902 7nhp Fowell traction engine pictured at Old Warden village, with the attractive village hall in the background.

A comparison between the working road locomotives and their proud sisters, the showman's engines, is well demonstrated here in a photograph taken at Eastnor Castle in May 2004. The showman's is 1904 Burrell 'Lady, Pride of England' and the road locomotives are the 1928 Fowler 'Atlas' and the 1910 Fowler no. 11111.

A 6-ton Aveling-Barford road roller from 1938 is seen resting after a road run outside a village pub in Warwickshire. This engine worked for Coventry City Council Parks Department.

Newcomen, a Dartmouth blacksmith, was the first to invent and install this relatively simple but effective machinery in mines.

However, the machinery was crude and costly in fuel, and in the mid-eighteenth century a Glasgow University scientist, James Watt, made crucial alterations to the Newcomen engine by enclosing the (previously open) cylinder, which in effect heralded the modern steam engine. James Watt was partnered by Matthew Boulton from Birmingham, and together they patented the Boulton and Watt steam engine, which had a virtual monopoly from then on both in mines and in factories, where the Boulton and Watt system of rotary shafts and pulleys would drive machinery until the nineteenth century, and so the steam age was born.

The first recorded steam vehicle – albeit somewhat crude – was built by a Frenchman, Nicholas Cugnot, in 1769 for military use; it is now preserved in Paris. The turn of the nineteenth century saw an explosion in steam use, initially with the railways. The talented Cornish inventor Richard Trevithick led the way in 1804, building 'Penydarren' for the Welsh tramroad. Trevithick also built a steam carriage which he demonstrated by driving to London in 1800; incredibly, however, this horseless carriage did not excite interest. From then on various inventors and

promoters built locomotives and opened railway lines, including the famous George Stephenson who in 1825 built 'Locomotion No. 1' for the Stockton and Darlington Railway. His company then built what is arguably the ancestor of them all, 'Rocket', for the 1829 Rainhill Trials held on the Liverpool and Manchester Railway.

It seems that the application of steam to road use took a back seat until the middle decades of the nineteenth century, as the railways rapidly developed. However, as the first half of the century progressed the idea that steam power could take to the roads and, especially, find a use in agriculture coalesced in the minds of Victorian engineers and entrepreneurs. Strangely enough, the great Victorian engineer, and builder of the Great Western Railway, Isambard Kingdom Brunel, actually came out against steam being used on the road, and prior to that his great rival George Stephenson had also considered and dismissed the idea.

The precursor to the traction engine was the portable steam engine, which had been in use for some time in agriculture by the middle of the nineteenth century. The very first were mounted on frames but wheels were added fairly quickly so the engines could be moved around the farm and on the roads by

horses or other animals. These very basic machines were paired with threshing machines or attached to other farm machinery such as woodcutters. They had an extremely long life and are to be found working for real in Third-World countries even today, having quite easily outlived all other forms of steam power, other than preservation.

Matters started moving in the 1830s as steam carriages took to the roads; these must have been quite disturbing to people used only to horses and oxen for land transport, and the roads of the day were little more than dirt tracks and poorly maintained in all but the major towns. And, of course, railways could be planned with reasonable gradients, whereas roads took in all forms of going.

It is believed that one of the first self-moving agricultural engines was produced by the locomotive builders E.B. Wilson of Leeds in 1849 and called 'The Farmer's Engine', though it won no orders. Into the story now stepped Kent farmer Thomas

Aveling, who in 1859 created a self-moving agricultural by modifying a Clayton and Shuttleworth portable engine. For this invention and for the creation of the famous engineering firm of Aveling & Porter, based first at Rochester, then at Strood, which produced all forms of steam engines, he can quite properly be called the 'Father of the Traction Engine'.

There were around ninety makers of steam engines in the United Kingdom, mostly in England with a few in Scotland. As might be expected, a large number of makers hailed from the farming communities that they served in East Anglia, especially Lincolnshire, with other concentrations of builders in Leeds, Kent (Aveling & Porter) and Hampshire. This being the era of Victorian expansion of Empire and then Commonwealth, Britain exported her steamers to all parts of the globe. Many, however, were produced in North America and Europe; some of these followed English practice, others catered for their countries' specialist needs.

The glorious era of steam power could not last as the internal-combustion engine took hold from 1900 onwards and especially after the First World War (1914–18), when development was rapid. By the mid-1920s the traction engine was being superseded in agricultural use, and many of the famous makers such as Burrell, Fowler, Marshall, Ruston & Hornsby, Aveling & Porter, McLaren, Fodens, Sentinel and Ransomes, Sims & Jeffries had either closed their doors, consolidated or moved into other branches of engineering by the start of the Second World War (1939–45). If one had a time machine, the 1920s must have been an interesting period as the horse, steam power and the internal-combustion engine all competed for agricultural and road patronage.

Steam power continued into the 1940s and a little beyond, the railways building and using steam locomotives in Britain until the 1960s (the last steam engine ran on British Railways' tracks in 1968). Steam wagons, usually Fodens or Sentinel, worked into the 1960s, road rollers continued up to the early 1970s in isolated areas, and showman's engines certainly worked at fairs in the 1950s. While real steam working disappeared around this time, the preservation movement started to gain a foothold in the 1950s.

I have very faint memories as a young lad in the late 1940s and early 1950s of a traction engine working a threshing machine at the farm in Warwickshire where my father worked; I assume it was hired from the agricultural engineers Bomford & Evershed of Salford Priors. I cannot remember very much about it, though if I close my eyes the noise, heat, dust and smell of hot oil still remains; eventually a Fordson tractor, in itself an important part of agricultural history, took over the duty. Better memories from the 1950s are of the local council's Aveling & Porter 10-tonner steam road roller, which my grandfather crewed, and the occasional ride on the footplate when the foreman was not present. These, of course, were the last knockings of road steam at work in this country as all had gone, apart from isolated pockets, by the 1960s.

Preservation took off from 1950 onwards as owners and clubs organized meetings for like-minded enthusiasts. These were nothing like the traction engine rallies of today where crowds are sometimes numbered in the tens of thousands, and all forms of classic machinery are seen together with other entertainment for the public. The original rallies were usually local affairs for owners such as Arthur Napper, whose enthusiasm promoted the traction engine movement. It was Napper who organized the famous 'Wager for Ale' in 1950 where two engines, his own 1902

Marshall traction engine 'Old Timer' and Miles Chetwynd-Stapylton's 1918 Aveling & Porter traction engine 'Ladygrove', raced against each other. This race, and subsequent rematches, achieved much publicity, caught the imagination of the public and nourished the fledgling movement. 2004 saw the fiftieth anniversary of the National Traction Engine Trust, which is the major organization for traction engine owners and enthusiasts. The Road Locomotive Society, founded in 1937, has worked since then to document the history – oral, written and photographic – of the road steam engine. Other specialist organizations cater for individual classes of engine such as the Road Roller Association, the Steam Plough Club and so on. The preservation movement in this country has managed to preserve around sixty makes from the heyday of the traction engine, and some 2,500 individual engines.

The enthusiast is also well catered for in museums, especially one-makers like the Charles Burrell Museum in its home town of Thetford, Norfolk, and the Long Shop Museum at Leiston, Suffolk, which is actually part of the 1853 Garrett works.

Hundreds of traction engine rallies are held in the summer months, from small village fairs with a couple of steamers in attendance to the greatest rally in the world, the Great Dorset Steam Fair held in late August/early September each year, where more than 200 engines attend over five days and crowds of a quarter of a million are known. This growth from the small, local events of the 1950s shows both how the movement has grown and also the public's great enthusiasm for preserved road steam. The profile of traction engines has also been raised by the late Fred Dibnah MBE, owner of two Aveling & Porter engines, through his television appearances and his promotion and enthusiasm for all things steam.

The purpose of this book is to present a pictorial record of the traction engine in its various forms together with historical information on each class. The following chapters describe portables, traction engines and tractors, road rollers, wagons and cars, ploughing engines, and road locomotives and showman's engines. The last two hundred years have seen the tentative beginnings of the steam era on road and rail, through its heyday with the Victorians and Edwardians, its gradual decline in the period between the World Wars to the vibrant preservation scene of the past fifty years. It seems that man's fascination with steam power, whether it be on the road, rail or on the water, is not easily overcome.

Malcolm Ranieri
April 2005

Chapter 1
Portables

THE steam portable engine was the forerunner of all traction engines and has been the most long-lived of all forms of steam power.

Napoleon Bonaparte said that Great Britain was 'a nation of shopkeepers', but he may have been more accurate had he described the nation as being one of farmers. A huge proportion of the population was employed on the land at the time Napoleon is supposed to have uttered those words. A farm in the early 1800s was vastly different from the machine-driven agriculture we see today. Labour was very cheap, plentiful and local to the farm: very often whole families were tied to the place where they worked by housing and agricultural employment, and not many people travelled more than a few miles from home. The industrial revolution was in its infancy and at that time had not affected the working patterns of the labourer or minor craftsman. The villages of the day were usually clustered near the farms or estates that provided employment for the uneducated majority, and most had the services required with village shops such as butchers and grocers all to hand, making trips outside to the nearest town rare and notable events.

The ready supply of labour meant that it was not economic for the farmer to lay out good money on new equipment, to say nothing of the inherent conservatism and resistance to change very often shown by the farming community. The task of threshing corn, for example, was carried out with flails in much the same, very labour-intensive, way it had been for many hundreds of years. Now a steam engine could be belted to a threshing drum. However, the only area in which manual threshing could not compete with steam power was in its speed; but if speed was not the key factor, and if the figures added up,

OPPOSITE: A working picture of the 1868 2½nhp Brown & May portable 'Little Dragon' belted to an apple press at the Marcle Rally in August 2004.

why change? Very often a sense of community prevailed as well: the introduction of machinery would inevitably mean less labour being required, and the community looked to the farmer to provide its livelihood.

The inventor Richard Trevithick was at the forefront of the development of steam power for agricultural use and from the first decade of the nineteenth century was supplying portable engines to work sugar mills in the West Indies, and a few in the United Kingdom. For the first four decades of the century, however, the use of steam power was slow to catch on because the cost for the small farmer was prohibitive. The majority of such work was carried out by contractors who purchased portables and moved these from farm to farm, usually by horse, a practice that survived until the end of the steam era.

One of the most famous names in agriculture now enters the picture, Ransomes of Ipswich. The founder, Robert Ransome (1753–1830), son of a Norfolk schoolmaster, was apprenticed to an ironmonger in Norfolk but soon acquired a small iron foundry and from this small beginning the firm that was to become Ransomes, Sims and Jeffries, Agricultural Engineers, sprang. While other manufacturers, such as Howden's, had produced very small numbers of portable engines, it was Ransomes who advanced the design of the portable so that at the 1842 Royal Show at Bristol a self-propelled model was available, including a lengthened chassis to attach a small threshing machine. The Royal Agricultural Society had been founded in 1839 to promote and advance the cause of agriculture, especially new methods of farming which, of course, included steam power. Their shows, first held in Oxford, drew innovative manufacturers and their products from all parts of the country. These shows, more than anything else in a world largely devoid of advertising, promoted the steam engine for agriculture.

Other famous firms promoted the portable such as Hornsby of Grantham and Clayton & Shuttleworth, the latter producing

the modern style of horizontal cylinder in place of the vertical cylinders that had been in use before, and various models of greater horsepower were made available to the farmer.

It was only really from the 1850s that the portable sold in large numbers, and from then on even the most conservative-minded farmer employed, either as an owner or hired from a contractor, a portable for driving a threshing drum, a chaff cutter or saw bench. Not just agriculture but also industries – such as quarrying, forestry, the utilities and manufacturing – used the ubiquitous portable to drive machinery or pumps.

One of the main advantages of a portable is its relative simplicity, which meant that even the uneducated farm labourers of the nineteenth century, more used to horses, could grasp the essentials of operation. This simplicity can be summed up as follows: a boiler with a built-in firebox, horizontal tubes like a locomotive's and a cylinder with a connecting rod that turns a crankshaft and so powers a wheel to which a belt is attached to

drive the machinery. Among its useful attributes, a portable could be steamed up and ready for work from cold in around half an hour, and it was relatively cheap to run – advertisements of the time quote an 8hp engine using only 4lb of coal per hour for each horsepower. Because of the portable's relative simplicity repairs could – at a pinch – be effected by the local blacksmith, though the actual boiler might have required specialist attention for safety reasons.

Thus the portable began the mechanization of the farm and once the innate conservatism of the farmer was dispelled its use expanded until it was unusual for a farm not to have a portable of some kind. This laid the foundation for all that followed, right up to the present day where labour is minimal and machines and computers are in charge. In fact, because of the world-wide demand for this type of engine the portable was produced by some manufacturers into the 1950s. Of course, the major disadvantage was always that movement was dependent on another source, in most cases the horse, but where a portable was based in one area for a specific purpose this was not a problem, hence its longevity.

Most of the well-known manufacturers produced portables as part of their portfolio of steam engines, manufacturers such as Charles Burrell & Sons, Wm. Foster & Co. Ltd, Richard Garrett & Sons Ltd, Marshall, Sons & Co. Ltd and, as we have seen, Ransomes and Hornsby. There was also a plethora of smaller manufacturers, who in some cases only turned out a handful of engines. A few examples of these survive such as Barrows & Stewart, Farmers Foundry, Edward Humphries & Co. Ltd, and W. Lampitt & Co. Approximately 400 portables exist in preservation in this country and can be seen belted to threshing machines or saw benches, efficiently doing what they were built for in some cases well over one hundred years ago.

An important adaptation of the portable engine was the steam-powered fire engine and fire pump, the mainstay of fire brigades for many years until the introduction of the internal-combustion engine to this service. All these appliances were horse-drawn and must have been a dramatic sight: horses at full gallop, the bell ringing and the steam engine hissing away with its red livery contrasting well with the brass and copper fittings – an impressive sight and sound. Two manufacturers in this country produced the appliances used by the fire brigades, and provided fire protection in some companies and estates: Merryweather Ltd, of whose products some seventy examples exist; and Shand-Mason Ltd, some fifty of whose engines exist. These delightful machines are in some cases still owned by fire brigades and are cherished pets to be brought out for display at rallies, either horse-drawn or pumping away.

The humble portables worked away, very often unnoticed, on farms or in industry, unable to rival their more glamorous sisters and the next step in the evolution of steam power, the traction engines. However, they have outlived all in terms of usefulness, and in some Third World countries the steam portable works to this day as a stationary engine, 150 years after it first appeared.

A very early 2½nhp portable engine of 1868 by Brown & May, seen at a rally at Worcester Racecourse in September 2001.

BELOW: *A 3nhp 1870 Barrows & Stewart portable engine, built at Banbury and seen here at the Banbury Rally in June 2000.*

ABOVE: *An interesting comparison at the 2002 Weeting Rally, between a 1½nhp 1888 Tuxford portable built at Boston and a 4nhp 1917 Ransomes, Sims & Jefferies portable, called 'Little Lucy', built at Ipswich.*

Ransomes, Sims & Jefferies

The founder of this celebrated agricultural engineering firm was Robert Ransome (1753–1830) who originally opened an ironmongery shop and iron foundry in Norwich, where he cast ploughshares and brass castings. Ransome moved to a foundry in Ipswich in 1789, where he later took out patents for plough parts in 1808. His son James became a partner in 1809 and the business now became Ransome & Son, making and selling ploughshares and other agricultural implements. Various family members joined the firm, and over the first three decades of the nineteenth century other implements and machinery such as lawnmowers and threshing machines were added to the product range.

The firm moved to new premises at Orwell Works, Ipswich, Suffolk, in 1849 where a thousand employees worked for the firm, Ransome having also gained railway work. William Sims joined the company in 1854 to progress to partner, as did John Jefferies in 1880, and the firm of Ransomes, Sims & Jefferies Ltd was born in 1884.

In 1841 a Ransomes portable had been built and in 1842 a self-propelled version was exhibited. Ransomes & May (May being a previous partner, who went on to found Brown & May) exhibited a portable engine at the Great Exhibition in 1851 and further development saw a traction engine, basically an enhanced portable, introduced in 1862. Stationary steam engines for various applications in coal mines, mills and factories were developed and built by Ransomes. During the 1870s export business grew, and steam engines were modified to burn other fuels than coal.

The 1880s saw 6 and 8nhp agricultural traction engines, hauling 10 tons for the smaller engine and up to 15 tons for the larger engine; these were also fitted with a governer to drive a thresher. Later in the decade the 'Colonial' traction engine was produced for haulage, direct ploughing and threshing, rated at 15–60nhp. Showman's engines were also built in very small numbers by Ransomes for hauling fairground equipment and generating electricity for lighting and rides.

The Heavy Motor Car Order 1904 allowed the firm to introduce a compound 5-ton steam tractor in the first decade of the twentieth century. Both overtype and undertype (*see* Chapter 4) steam wagons were built by Ransomes, usually 5-ton compound, with various bodies, predominately flats and tippers. Ransomes did not manufacture road rollers, but they did design and build an experimental roller, a convertible, in 1907, though nothing came of this.

After the First World War, as the internal-combustion engine was replacing steam, Ransomes combined with Ruston & Hornsby of Lincoln to standardize designs and benefit from mass production. A new overtype steam wagon was produced in 1920, but by this time road steam was in decline and the last wagon was built in 1927, for export.

During this time Ransomes had been experimenting with and building oil engines and also internal combustion-engined farm machinery including tractors and cultivators, so were well placed as steam power became old-fashioned. However, steam engines were still built in small numbers and the last traction engine was sold as late as 1934, portables also continuing through the 1930s and 1940s. The association with Ruston & Hornby ended in 1940 when that firm formed an alliance with Davey, Paxman & Co. of Colchester. Ransomes sold the steam engine side of their business to Robey & Co. in Lincoln in 1956, so ending their long association with steam power.

In 1966 the firm moved to a new works at Nacton and the Orwell Works was sold in 1968. In 1987 the Electrolux Group bought the farm machinery division and now trade under the name of Agrolux. Finally, in 1998 Textron acquired Ransomes plc and became Textron Turf Care & Specialty Products, changing the name in 2001 to Textron Golf, Turf and Specialty Products.

Around 140 Ransomes, Sims & Jefferies Ltd engines are preserved, mostly the portables and traction engines that were the backbone of the business, including a very early traction engine of 1882, and a rare wagon that has been imported from Australia.

ABOVE: *A large, 12nhp Marshall portable built in 1916 at Gainsborough, and seen at the June 2000 rally at Banbury.*

LEFT: *A 2nhp portable built in 1898 by Barrows & Co. Ltd (successors to Barrows & Stewart) at Banbury and pictured here at Avoncroft Museum at Bromsgrove.*

Clayton & Shuttleworth Ltd

The engineering firm of Clayton, Shuttleworth & Co. was established by Joseph Shuttleworth and Nathaniel Clayton in 1842, at Stamp End Works, Lincoln. Clayton & Shuttleworth were early producers of the portable steam engine, the first being built in 1845; it is said to have been similar to the design of William Howden of Boston, Lincolnshire, who is credited with the first complete working portable engine. The humble portable engine formed an important part of production throughout the life of the company.

Thomas Aveling is credited with the invention of the self-propelled portable, or fledgling traction engine, but several manufacturers also produced this type of steam engine around 1860, including Clayton & Shuttleworth. As Clayton & Shuttleworth manufactured prototypes and complete engines for several inventors in their early days, especially Aveling and Fowler, one can assume that they used the knowledge so gained to produce their own designs. The 1860 Clayton & Shuttleworth was a portable engine with single gearing added and a pilot wheel at the front with steersman and detachable tender, doubling up as a water tender. By the mid-1870s Clayton & Shuttleworth were producing the standard form of all-geared, integral-tender, steerage traction engine with a normal footplate, for the agricultural market; in Lincoln the firm was ideally placed to serve East Anglia and its farming community.

The firm diversified to build, among other engineering products, a few Clayton tram engines, small vertical boilered stationary engines, and eventually steam shunting locomotives, of 0-4-0 design in various gauges. In the early 1900s, in response to the Heavy Motor Car Order of 1904, the steam tractor was produced, with rear suspension springing, in single and compound versions. In addition to the range of portable engines, traction engines, tractors and wagons, steam road rollers were produced from the early 1900s, and a handful of showman's road locomotives.

A subsidiary company called Clayton Wagons Ltd was set up at the start of the First World War, at Abbey Works in Lincoln, originally for railway work. At this works steam wagons, at first overtype and then undertype (*see* Chapter 4), were produced in good numbers, and were successful. The Abbey Works also produced steam railway locomotives for domestic and overseas customers.

Clayton & Shuttleworth Ltd, as it was eventually known, was absorbed into the famous firm of Marshall, Sons & Co. Ltd in 1929, the engineering side having already been hived off to Babcock & Wilcox Ltd in 1924. At the time of writing thirty-three traction engines, nineteen portable engines, eleven road rollers and three wagons have been preserved.

A 1919 Clayton & Shuttleworth portable seen at the Holcot Rally in August 2001.

21

An unidentified Ruston & Hornsby portable belted to a small saw bench at the Roxton Rally in September 1991.

TOP LEFT: *A 5nhp 1935 portable built by Ransomes, Sims & Jefferies of Ipswich, keeping company with a Fordson Major tractor at the Marcle Rally in July 2000.*

TOP RIGHT: *The fate of many portable engines when their work has been done: a Clayton & Shuttleworth languishes at a farm in the village of Hartest, Suffolk in May 2000.*

A 1905 Shand-Mason Ltd fire engine which originally worked at the War Department's Curragh Camp in Ireland. It is seen here pumping water at the Knowl Hill Rally in August 1998.

Highley Station on the Severn Valley Railway in June 2000: a 1901 Shand-Mason fire engine named 'Florian', pulled by two shire horses and with the crew in period uniform; this engine is owned by Sutton Coldfield Fire Service.

OPPOSITE: *An 1899 Shand-Mason fire engine, named 'Newbury', at the July 2001 Weeting Rally.*

An 1890 Merryweather Ltd fire engine, called 'Blenheim', at the June 2000 Banbury Rally. This engine is owned by the Warwickshire Fire & Rescue Service and kept at Shipston-on-Stour Fire Station.

Chapter 2
Traction Engines – Agricultural and Tractors

TRACTION ENGINES were either 'agricultural', used in farming, or 'general purpose', used in areas such as haulage. This chapter also covers a spin-off from the traction engine, the steam tractor, which as we shall see was used primarily for light-haulage duties.

While the genesis of the steam traction engine can be traced through the 18th-century beam engines, the road steamers and portables of the early nineteenth century, and the genius of inventor engineers like Newcomen, Trevithick and Watt, one man stands out from all the others: Thomas Aveling. Aveling has been called the 'Father of the Traction Engine'. He was born in 1824 in Cambridgeshire and had an unhappy childhood, but while apprenticed to a farmer in his home county he showed his mechanical ability in repairing farm machinery. This was the making of the man and he soon began farming in his own right. His aptitude for all things mechanical bore fruit when he opened his own engineering firm in Rochester, Kent, in 1850, where he concentrated on the provision of mechanized power for agriculture.

In Chapter 1 we saw that up to that time farming in Britain was very labour intensive, but steam power was gradually becoming established in the countryside. The portable steam engine relied on (usually) horse power to move from location to location and Aveling is quoted as saying 'it is an insult to mechanical science to see half a dozen horses dragging along a steam engine'!

The first reported self-moving agricultural engine was produced by locomotive builders E.B. Wilson of Leeds in 1849, though it appears nothing came of this. In 1859 Thomas Aveling created a self-moving agricultural steam engine by modifying a Clayton & Shuttleworth portable engine with a driving chain between crankshaft and axle, though steering was still carried out by a horse between the forward shafts. It may seem strange to us, with the benefit of 150 or so years' hindsight, that steering should cause a problem; but this was in the age of the horse, either on its own or attached to a cart or carriage, and in all cases steered by reins. However, Aveling and other manufacturers soon did away with the horse, initially replacing it with a wheel on a bracket and levers, and what was called 'pilot steerage'.

Aveling had collaborated with Clayton & Shuttleworth of Lincoln to produce engines in the first instance because he did not have the necessary manufacturing resources, but in 1861 he began to produce his own engines from his Rochester factory, eventually relocating to premises at Strood. These engines sold for £360: a tidy sum in those days.

It was around 1865 that the steering problem was finally resolved by the method we see today of chain-and-bobbin steering worked from the footplate. Aveling and the other manufacturers then improved the self-propelled engine by changing the final drive from chains – which proved unreliable – to a gear drive. Who knows: if the chain technology of today could have been employed then, all traction engines might have used chain final drive.

OPPOSITE: The 6nhp 1922 Burrell traction engine 'Susie' at the Lister Tyndale Rally in June 2004, with North Nibley Church in the background.

Other areas where engineering science was applied were springing, especially to the rear of the engine, and differential gears. Water tanks became an integral part of the engine, rather than a separate tender as seen in the early machines produced by Savages of King's Lynn. 'Compounding' to make more efficient use of steam was one of the next steps, finally resolved in 1881 by Aveling and also Fowlers. This is the routing of steam leaving the high-pressure cylinder to a lower-pressure cylinder, much used on the railways to maximize the efficient use of power in locomotives. However, not all manufacturers made compound machines as there was a demand for the simpler 'single' for operational purposes. Thus the traction engine evolved into the machine that we see today in preservation.

While Aveling was a brilliant engineer, development work was carried out at all the competing factories as the use of traction engines in agriculture and other areas expanded. Other well-known manufacturers at the forefront of design were Charles Burrell & Sons Ltd, whose claim was that their engines were hand-built and no two alike; John Fowler & Co. (Leeds) Ltd, the firm to become famous for its ploughing engines; Richard Garrett & Sons Ltd of Leiston, another general supplier of all forms of steam engine; and Marshall, Sons & Co. Ltd of Gainsborough. Most of these makers – and many more – were linked to the countryside, the natural habitat of the traction engine, and had been either farmers or agricultural engineers before turning to the production of steam engines. Many of these firms also supplied the machinery powered by the traction engine, such as threshing drums, chaff cutters, saw benches and so on: firms like Ransomes, Sims & Jefferies; Clayton & Shuttleworth; Marshall, Sons & Co. Ltd and Charles Burrell & Sons Ltd. All produced a complete package for the farmer or contractor.

The mention of the contractor is important in the history of the traction engine. The cost of an engine and machinery such as a threshing drum could be prohibitive, especially for the smaller farmer. Some jobs like threshing only took place over a short period in the farming year, and to have machinery standing idle the rest of the time was unacceptable. Therefore, contractors multiplied as the engines benefited from development and became more reliable. A threshing contractor would visit farms in all but the summer months with his engine, threshing drum, straw elevator and chaff cutter, and would be accompanied by a driver and labourer; the farmer usually supplied coal, water and any other labour required. The visit of the contractor was an event much anticipated by the farm and local village, especially the children, and old-time countrymen often recall steam threshing with affection as one of the highlights of the year.

Contractors also realized that traction engines could be more versatile now they were self-propelled. When not on threshing duty engines might work in forestry, belted to a saw bench or pulling out tree stumps (for which Fowlers actually manufactured an implement), driving water pumps or, of course, in haulage. All manner of goods was carried behind traction engines: coal, timber, bricks, quarried material, farm produce, manufactured goods and so on. Manufacturers recognized this new area and built bespoke carts and wagons.

A 3nhp, 3-ton Wallis & Steevens tractor (works no. 2593) of 1902 belonging to Joseph Redford, a contractor based in Turnford, Hertfordshire. It is pictured carrying a covered load through the streets of London in the early part of the twentieth century.

A 6nhp Marshall traction engine, reg. no. DV 7341 (works no. 85890), belted to agricultural machinery in her working days. This engine is now preserved.

RIGHT: A delightful working picture of a 1905 4nhp Tasker 'Little Giant' (works no. 1365) tractor on the road. The engine was operated by Tasker themselves; the trailer carries a tilt bearing the company name, so this photograph may record a demonstration run.

It is here that the steam tractor comes into the story. This lighter version of the traction engine was developed around 1890, specifically to compete against the looming threat of internal combustion-engined lorries to carry lighter loads over sometimes shorter distances. This light traction was facilitated by the Heavy Motor Car Act of 1903 and subsequent 1904 Orders, which allowed traction engines under 5 tons to travel at speeds not exceeding 5mph (8km/h), and to be driven by one man. These were popular with contractors, and timber hauliers particularly took to them; local authorities also were users as some were built as convertibles and so could double up as a road roller. In 1923 the next Heavy Motor Car Act specified an increase in maximum weight to 7¼ tons, allowing greater haulage by steam, and some manufacturers took advantage of this to produce bigger tractors. By this time, however, the writing was on the wall and the internal combustion-engined motor lorry eventually swept all before it. Many steam-based contractors could not compete and were bankrupted, and even the railways felt the effect of the road haulage on their freight business.

Preservation after the Second World War onward meant that traction engines were rescued from dereliction or bought out of service (some farmers still used them, sticking to the old ways), and renovated by enthusiasts. Traction engines and tractors are probably the best known of all steam road engines, and around thirty manufacturers are represented in preservation. The bulk of them from the famous makers of Allchin, Aveling & Porter,

Burrell, Clayton & Shuttleworth, Davey Paxman, Fodens (better known for its wagons), Foster, Fowell, Fowler, Garrett, Mann, Marshall, McLaren, Ransomes, Robey, Rustons, Tasker, and Wallis & Steevens. There are some rare survivors and one-offs like the John Collings hand-built engine of 1910, the 1891 Gibbons & Robinson, the 1872 Howard traction engine, the 1887 W. Lampitt & Co. chain-driven engine, the Robinson & Auden of 1900, and the Savage traction engine of 1889, this last company being better known for its centre engines in fairground rides.

While this book concentrates on the builders in Great Britain, traction engines were manufactured in their thousands overseas, especially America, where names like Advance-Rumeley, Avery, Buffalo-Pitts, Case (still trading – its diesel tractors are sold all over the world), Minneapolis and Waterloo are as well known in preservation in the USA as our own Aveling & Porter or Burrell. A few examples of American hardware have reached Great Britain and can occasionally be seen at rallies. Also, while Great Britain exported her engines to many continental countries and to her then colonies, especially Australia and New Zealand, Europe also produced steam engines, sometimes to British design or patent.

In the middle of the nineteenth century Thomas Aveling started a movement which was an undoubted success in the mechanization of agriculture in this country, and helped to make Britain the power it became in Victorian times.

TOP LEFT: *A 7nhp 1910 Allchin traction engine named 'Evedon Lad' on a road run at Hunsbury Hill, Northampton in April 1996; these engines were built at Northampton.*

ABOVE: *Road and rail steam come together at Toddington Station on the Gloucestershire Warwickshire Railway on the occasion of their Steam Rally in October 2002. The 1899 6nhp Aveling & Porter traction engine 'Queen Victoria' looks on as Great Western Railway no. 6960 'Raveningham Hall' passes by.*

An 8nhp 1905 Allchin traction engine named 'Lena' at the Delapre Gates in Northampton – where the firm took many of its publicity pictures – during the April 1996 road run.

ABOVE: *An 1899 Aveling & Porter traction engine is captured at night with her living van on tow at the August 2004 Kemble Rally.*

TOP LEFT: *The 6nhp 1917 Burrell traction engine 'Charlie B' basks in the early morning sunshine at the Great Dorset Steam Fair in September 1994.*

BELOW LEFT: *The 6nhp, 1901 Burrell traction engine 'Ted Haggard' poses outside a barn on the Hatton Country World farm estate, and really looks the part of agricultural steam, in May 2004 during the National Traction Engine Trust's 'hands-on' weekend.*

BELOW: *A 1901 Burrell traction engine about to be belted to the saw bench in the working area at the July 1999 Weeting Rally.*

At the Great Dorset Steam Fair in September 1994 the 7nhp 1899 Burrell traction engine 'Endurance' is belted to a threshing machine in the working area.

A rare pairing: the early 8nhp 1886 Burrell traction engine
'Marina' and a threshing machine also built by Burrell enjoy
the morning sunshine at Weeting in July, 1998.

A 1913 Burrell traction engine from New Zealand at the
Welland Rally in July 2001 demonstrates the sort of work
she would have carried out in bygone days, hitched to a
trailer loaded with logs.

The 8nhp 1909 Burrell traction engine 'Keeling', and a living van, standing outside the Crown Inn at Ampney Crucis in the Cotswolds in August 1995, during a road run. This engine was used for threshing, haulage and logging until to 1954 before passing into preservation.

BELOW LEFT: A 5nhp 1925 Foster traction engine is pictured on a road run at Leonard Stanley, near Stonehouse, Gloucestershire in 2002. Clearly seen in this picture is the outline of the firm's tanks, which forms part of the emblem on the smokebox.

BELOW RIGHT: The firm of Foden is best known for its wagons, but it also built traction engines; this is a 7nhp 1912 version called 'Wattie Pollock', pictured in the working area at the 1993 Great Dorset Steam Fair.

The 7nhp 1920 Foster traction engine 'Viscountess Rhondda' at the June 2000 Stoke Row Rally.

TOP RIGHT: A 6nhp Fowler traction engine of 1915 named 'Lord of the Isles' turning into the rally site at Leighton Buzzard in May 1998.

The St Ives firm of Fowell were a low-volume producer of engines; here one of their products, a 8nhp traction engine of 1913 named 'Cromwell', is seen on a road run with a living van in Framlingham, Suffolk. It is followed, in a vintage traffic-jam recreation, by a 1930 Foden wagon fitted with a pantechnicon body.

A 7nhp Garrett traction engine of 1909 named 'Margaret', being prepared to work a threshing machine at the August 2001 Holcot Rally in Northamptonshire.

A 6nhp Fowler of 1895 named 'Endurance' stands outside the Sheffield Park Station of the preserved Bluebell Railway.

Richard Garrett & Sons Ltd

This firm has a long and varied history, dating back to 1778 when the first Richard Garrett set up as a bladesmith in Leiston, Suffolk. His son, also Richard, took over the business in 1805 and it was his son, also Richard (1807–66), who started the manufacture of a long line of steam engines when he took over the firm in the 1830s.

The first engines built under the third Richard Garrett were fixed steam engines and the firm also started development work on threshing machines, for which they would become renowned. Garrett's built not just threshing machines for the agricultural market but also all manner of farm equipment such as seed drills, ploughs, reaping machines, saw benches and so on.

Portable steam engines were first produced in 1848, and ten years later the first traction engine was built, originally under licence to Avelings, then in 1876 to Garrett's own design. This original gear-driven traction engine was only built for three years due to market problems in agriculture, but manufacture restarted in 1895 and continued to the end of steam production in 1931.

The late Victorian and early Edwardian period saw Garrett move into the other fields of steam-engine manufacture. The firm's first steam road roller, a 10-tonner, was built in 1898, though later on light 4+ tonners and heavy rollers up to 18 tons were also built, and a large number exported to Europe and the Far East. A number of ploughing engines were built at the turn of the twentieth century for the German market and also for New Zealand. Road locomotives, some of which became showman's, were also built in small numbers from 1903, principally for haulage contractors.

The Garrett model 4CD steam tractor, a very attractive and versatile machine, was built from 1905 in 3 and 4nhp versions; early models were single-cylindered but compounding came into use later. To combat the march of the internal combustion-engined tractor in farming, Garretts also built in 1917 a lightweight steam tractor, with the boiler at the rear and steerage at the front, for direct ploughing; this was called the 'Suffolk Punch', after the local heavy horse. However, this was really too late to stem the tide and only eight were built, though luckily one example has been preserved.

Overtype steam wagons were built from 1909, though experiments had been made beforehand with an undertype wagon – most of these were 3- or 5-tonners (*see* Chapter 4 for the distinction between over- and undertype). The wagons could be had in all types: flats, tippers, vans, specialist bodies, trailers and so on, and were built until 1924. A 6-ton overtype wagon was launched in 1926 but failed to gain sales. Persevering with the steam-wagon market, Garrett built some undertype four-wheel wagons as 4-, 6- and 8-tonners, and this design continued until the

end of manufacture in 1930. A total of 995 steam wagons of all types were built. This may not be comparable with Fodens or Sentinel, but was certainly significant. Four have been preserved, including an early version from 1912.

Garrett diversified into the building of electric vehicles after the First World War, such as trolley buses sold to local authorities. Continuing the local-authority theme, refuse vehicles were also constructed in the 1920s. Other engineering products poured from the factory: agricultural equipment continued to be made; diesel tractors were built in small numbers; during both world wars armaments and Army vehicles were built; machine tools and even esoteric machinery like petrol pumps were manufactured – nothing seemed too much trouble to be taken on by this remarkable firm.

Like many of the steam-engineering firms, Garretts were forced by market problems to join the combine Agricultural & General Engineers Ltd; when this collapsed in 1932, the original Garrett family firm died with it. The Leiston works was taken over by Beyer, Peacock & Co. Ltd, railway locomotive builders of Manchester, and a new company was formed in 1932 called the Richard Garrett Engineering Works Ltd; after a varied history from the 1960s the works closed in 1978.

Around 22,500 steam engines were built by this firm, 20,000 being portable engines. In preservation, approximately 120 are still extant of all types, including a solitary ploughing engine. The Long Shop (for the building of portable engines) at Leiston, part of the works, has been restored and is now a museum of Garrett machinery and memorabilia.

The earliest preserved Garrett traction engine, a 6nhp model built in 1902 and named 'Lucy', approaching Broadway, Worcestershire as it pulls a cart on its way to the Gloucestershire Warwickshire Railway Steam Fair in August 1998.

The earliest preserved traction engine from Richard Hornsby & Sons is this 8nhp 1889 engine. It is pictured here on the road run from the Gloucestershire Warwickshire Railway Steam Rally in September 2003, with Stanway Hall as a backdrop.

BELOW LEFT: The 6nhp 1911 Garrett traction engine 'Olive' is unusual in that she is superheated, as can clearly be seen from the cover on top of the smokebox. She is pictured here at the Bedfordshire Rally in September, 2003.

BELOW RIGHT: The 6nhp Marshall traction engine 'Jimmy B' being prepared at Holcot Farm in order to take part in the National Traction Engine Trust's 50th Anniversary Road Run around Northamptonshire in September 2004.

Marshall, Sons & Co. Ltd

The founder of this famous firm was a man called William Marshall, from an old Gainsborough family, originally an overseas agent for the Manchester firm of millwrights and steam-engine builders of William Fairbairn & Sons. In 1842 he branched out on his own and purchased the defunct engineering works of William Garland & Son at Back Street Foundry in Gainsborough. Six years later the works was renamed Britannia Ironworks, and the first of a long line of beautifully engineered road steam engines was built. The works was expanded in 1856 as business picked up, and the two sons of William became partners in 1857 (James) and 1861 (Henry), hence the firms title Marshall, Sons & Co., though the founder died in 1861.

Marshalls were noted for their steam portable engines from 1860, and gold medals were won around the world for the portables. If the company badge proudly displayed on the boilers of the many preserved engines is scrutinized, one will see these medals reproduced for all to see – an early form of brand advertisement.

The steam portables were built in various and versatile forms, dependent on the requirements of the industry. Both vertical and horizontal boilers were produced, the former being of power ratings from 1½–12nhp and the latter from 10–35nhp.

Later variations of portable included undertypes, overtypes and semi-portables, and power classifications ranged from 8–60nhp. These were very often anything but portable and would be mounted in situ for a job of work in industry or agriculture. These engines were sold all over the world in huge numbers, especially the Marshall class L, a horizontal design that could be had in many combinations and power classifications, and the vertical-type class MP. These engines were often custom-built to operate in an environment where coal or even wood was not available, fireboxes being adapted to burn any form of by-product such as sawdust, straw, seed husks and so on. Economy was also a byword and the firm proudly proclaimed at one time that their engines were 'the most economical steam engines in the world'.

The first traction engine came from the firm in 1876, and was unusual in that the engine and motion were undermounted below the boiler. This type did not last long, and five years later the so-called 'improved traction engine' was produced by Marshall, the engine and motion being more conventionally mounted on top of the boiler, much as we see in the products of other firms. Development work on the firm's traction engines did not lag behind that on its portables and semi-portables, and while the single-cylinder type was favoured, compounding was also used, especially for heavy haulage.

Marshall also produced agricultural machinery to work with the portable or traction engine. Their threshing machines, in particular, could be seen at work all over the country and in preservation are a common sight at rallies, belted to all manner of power. Marshalls were also specialists in the field of tea-making machinery from the late 1870s due to a partnership with the Jackson Brothers, tea planters in Assam, India.

Marshall produced fine steam road rollers from the 1900s onwards, in the conventional, horizontal boiler, form from 6- to 16-ton size, and later with compounding, but also the Millars-Marshall tandem steam roller with a vertical boiler, developed for quick-reverse action on hot asphalt. As with other manufacturers, the Heavy Motor Car Orders 1904 prompted Marshall to build a 5-ton steam tractor, fitted with two or three speeds, as required, which immediately found favour with hauliers.

From the turn of the century Marshalls trialled paraffin- and oil-fired tractors, and saw the potential of the internal-combustion engine for agricultural and other work, and during the First World War the factory produced armaments. From 1929 the company became part of the Thomas W. Ward empire, and from 1946 reformed as Marshall-Fowler, and the famous Field Marshall series of tractors were born. At the time of writing the firm forms part of the TWR Group as Track Marshall.

The last steam portable engines and steam road rollers were made in the mid-1940s by Marshalls, and the firm's long life is reflected in the numbers of their products preserved: some 350 steam engines. As might be expected, portable engines and traction engines account for two thirds of those, with around 120 of each type preserved.

This 7nhp Marshall traction engine of 1915 is pictured at night outside a redundant aircraft hangar in July 2003 at the Kemble Rally.

TOP LEFT: *This 7nhp Marshall traction engine of 1913 is taking part in a road run in October 2003, and is seen at Little Chalfont in the Chilterns.*

TOP RIGHT: *This traction engine has entered the folklore of preservation: it is the 6nhp 1902 Marshall traction engine named 'Old Timer' originally owned by the famous Arthur Napper. His inspired races, the so-called 'wager for ale', kick-started the movement. 'Old Timer' is seen here on her way to the 2003 Stoke Row Rally.*

The 6nhp 1893 McLaren traction engine 'Phoenix', with cart and living van, on a road run at Chalford in Gloucestershire.

TOP LEFT: *The 6nhp 1904 Ransome, Sims & Jefferies traction engine 'Lady Diana' on a road run at Toddington, Gloucestershire in October 2003.*

TOP RIGHT: *This 6nhp Ransome, Sims & Jefferies traction engine of 1915 is pictured at the 2004 Welland Rally with the Malvern Hills in the background.*

The 7nhp 1916 Ransome, Sims & Jefferies traction engine 'Mendip Lady' pictured in its home town of Ipswich during the Great Eastern Road Run of May 1999, passing through the Ipswich Docks.

This splendid 5nhp Robey traction engine of 1908, named 'Pride of the Walk', had just been restored when she was pictured at the 2004 Welland Rally.

BELOW LEFT: The only known Robinson & Auden Ltd traction engine from 1900, a 6nhp version named 'Little Buttercup'; it is pictured in September 2004 at the Bedfordshire Rally.

BELOW RIGHT: The unique 1889 Savage Bros Ltd 7nhp traction engine 'Elisa'. While a number of other products of this firm are preserved, this is the only original road steamer preserved (there are two full-size replicas); it is pictured at the Banbury Rally in June 2003.

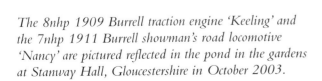

This 7nhp Wallis & Steevens traction engine named 'The Reeder Express' is belted to a Ransome, Sims & Jefferies threshing machine at the June 1994 Burbage Rally.

The 8nhp 1909 Burrell traction engine 'Keeling' and the 7nhp 1911 Burrell showman's road locomotive 'Nancy' are pictured reflected in the pond in the gardens at Stanway Hall, Gloucestershire in October 2003.

The 6nhp 1901 Burrell traction engine 'Ted Haggard' working a saw bench at the Castle Combe Rally in May 1993.

TOP LEFT: The 7nhp 1904 Clayton & Shuttleworth traction engine 'Old Glory' is seen here at the Belvoir Castle Rally in Leicestershire in May 2004.

LEFT: A 6nhp 1914 Robey traction engine at Engine Hill, Porthowen, Cornwall, on the occasion of the West of England Steam Engine Society's road run in August 1995.

The 8nhp 1907 Burrell traction engine 'Dreadnought' pictured amongst the chaff from the threshing machine she is belted to at the Weeting Rally in June 1998. Though this is a re-creation, it is a typical scene that could have been seen anywhere in the country in the heyday of agricultural steam.

TOP RIGHT: This 4nhp Aveling & Porter tractor, built in 1907 and named 'Queen of Herts', is pictured on the approaches to Leighton Buzzard in June 2000. This engine was built as a tractor but fitted with rear rollers in 1928; it has now reverted back to tractor wheels.

The 7nhp 1909 Burrell traction engine 'Victory' working a stone crusher at Astwood Bank, Worcestershire in May 1993.

The unique Brown & May tractor from 1909 is seen at the National Traction Engine Trust's 50th Anniversary Gathering at Hollowell, Northamptonshire in September 2004.

The 4nhp 1927 Burrell Gold Medal tractor 'Tinkerbell' is seen here at the Waddesdon Rally in September 1992. The engines are called 'Gold Medal' because Burrell was the only firm to be awarded one for all-round efficiency at the 1908 RAC trials.

A 4nhp John Collings tractor, built in 1910 and named 'Bacton Hall', seen at the July 1999 Weeting Rally working area. This small family works, located at Bacton Hall in Norfolk, only produced three engines; no. 2, seen here, is the only survivor.

This 3nhp Fowler tractor, built in 1920 and named 'Lord Doverdale', at the Belvoir Castle Rally in May 2004. This engine was purchased new by Olive Partington of Glossop, Derbyshire for haulage of timber logs from the railway station to the Turn Lee Mill paper works, and worked until 1960.

BELOW LEFT: This 3nhp tractor was built in 1904 by Wm. Foster & Co. Ltd. The type was called the Wellington tractor and is seen newly restored at the Bedfordshire Rally in September 2003.

BELOW RIGHT: A 1920 4nhp Garrett tractor is seen on a road run at Blakedown, Leamington Spa, Warwickshire.

TOP LEFT: *The 4nhp 1913 Garrett tractor 'Mr Potter' transports a water tanker on a road run in July 2004, in connection with the Great Bucks Steam Working at Ickford.*

TOP RIGHT: *The 4nhp 1920 Garrett tractor 'Princess Mary' outside the barns at Hatton Country World farm estate in May 2004, at the National Traction Engine Trust's 'hands-on' weekend. This engine was built for the War Department and later converted to showman's specification for Jarvis, South Wales, eventually being sold for timber haulage work in the late 1930s.*

LEFT: *This 4nhp tractor built in 1919 and nicknamed 'The Joker' is the sole surviving example of the 'Suffolk Punch' built by Garrett; it is pictured here at the 1992 Great Dorset Steam Fair. Eight of these rear-boilered, front-steerage tractors were built in a vain attempt to stem the tide of the internal-combustion engine in agriculture.*

The 4nhp 1921 Marshall tractor 'Glenys' is a convertible (to roller, if required). Here it is seen with living van at the Rempstone Rally in July 1992.

BELOW LEFT: The 5-ton 1918 Mann tractor 'Lizer' runs round the site at the Marcle Rally in July 2000. This engine was sold new to John Jones of Tintern, Gwent, for use in his sawmill. In 1947 it was purchased for £25 by a Mr Knight, marine engineer, whose family kept her for fifty years, on loan during that time to the Bressingham Steam Museum; in 1997 it was bought by the Hopkins family of Newport.

BELOW RIGHT: An example of the Tasker 'Little Giant' series of 4nhp tractors, seen here at the Great Dorset Steam Fair in September 2003.

Ruston & Hornsby Ltd

This firm is an amalgamation of two well-known steam manufacturers. Richard Hornsby was an iron and brass founder working from a foundry at Spittlegate Ironworks, Grantham in 1815, and became quite grandly 'agricultural implement makers, iron and brass founder, and paper maker' by 1850. His three sons joined the firm and in 1851 the company became Richard Hornsby & Sons, the founder dying in 1864. In 1880 the firm gained limited liability company status, and then in 1918 came the amalgamation.

The second part of the story begins in 1840 with 'millwrights and engineers' Proctor & Burton from Lincoln. Joseph Ruston became a partner in 1857, the firm becoming Ruston, Proctor & Co. and, like Hornsby, they achieved limited liability status in 1899, titled Ruston, Proctor & Co. Ltd. The amalgamation between these two steam and general engineering companies came in 1918, and the firm became Ruston & Hornsby Ltd. The works was at Sheaf Iron Works, Lincoln.

The first steam portable from Richard Hornsby was produced in 1849, and in 1863 the first traction engine was built, showing a great deal of railway locomotive influence, and few were made. More conventional traction engines were produced at Hornsby from 1880, offered in 5, 6, 8, 10 and 12nhp versions, the maker calling them 'improved patent narrow-gauge agricultural locomotive or traction engine'. Portable and stationary steam engines of all types were offered in many different nhp ratings, and sold well. Hornsby also built a tramway locomotive adapted from their traction engine, and winding engines for mining applications. However, oil engines became their main production from 1892, steam being slowly phased out and finally stopping in 1906.

Ruston, Proctor & Co., like Hornsby, developed and sold the steam portable engine from the mid-Victorian period onwards.

Their first traction engines appeared in 1876; these were conventional single-cylinder and duplex-cylinder types, the former in 6, 7, 8 and 10nhp ratings, the latter in 8 and 10nhp versions. Ruston, Proctor & Co. also made railway locomotives of 0–4–0 configuration, mainly for contractor's use, the first being made in 1867. The Great Eastern Railway were supplied with 0–6–0 tank locomotives in 1868, three being turned into crane engines.

Like Hornsby, Ruston produced stationary engines of all types – horizontal and vertical boilers, single and compound – for use in factories, mills and as winding engines for mining. Ruston also produced a 5-ton steam tractor, the model SCD, a two-speed vehicle able to move loads of 7 tons.

Perhaps one of the best known of Ruston products was the 'steam navvy', a vertical-boilered excavator for digging and moving stone in quarries. These were very successful, hundreds being sold all over the world. Ruston & Hornsby went on to build heavy oil-engine-driven excavators, based on Ruston, Proctor & Co.'s expertise with the 'steam navvy'.

The Lincoln works of Ruston & Hornsby took over the steam engineering side and produced a fine range of steam road rollers, and also continued with steam tractors, especially the fine 'Lincoln Imp', and portables and traction engines, the last of which was built in 1936. The oil-engine side of the new firm was dealt with at Grantham. In 1940, Ruston & Hornsby amalgamated with Davey, Paxman & Co. Ltd of Colchester.

Richard Hornsby & Sons has fourteen examples in preservation: portables from 1870 and three traction engines up to 1903. Ruston, Proctor & Co. Ltd has over fifty examples including portables, tractors, traction engines and a handful of road rollers. The amalgamated firm of Ruston & Hornsby Ltd has forty portables, tractors, traction engines and road rollers preserved, including a unique 1919 roller powered by a Nuffield diesel engine.

A 4nhp 1919 Garrett type 4CD tractor steams away gently in a corner of the Rushmoor Rally in July 1998.

This is an example of the Ruston & Hornsby 'Lincoln Imp' type, here seen with matching vintage cart. This is a 4nhp tractor built in 1918 and was photographed at Leigh Sinton Farm, Worcestershire in December 2003. This engine was actually built by Ruston, Proctor & Co. Ltd, but delivered by the successor company, Ruston & Hornsby. It is now owned by Andrew Semple, Chairman of the NTET.

The 4nhp 1930 Wallis & Steevens tractor 'Duke of Wellington' is seen at the Leighton Buzzard Rally in May 2002.

Chapter 3
Road Rollers

THE best-known steam engines today are the steam road rollers, and the general public consistently refers to today's modern internal combustion-powered road rollers as 'steam rollers', which shows how much the steam-powered versions ingrained themselves into the public consciousness! This is because, though few have worked for real for forty years or more, if you discount rally re-creations, the steam road roller was a common sight on our roads from Victorian times. The road roller was the one traction engine that the public could regularly see in action, sometimes just outside the front door, rolling the tarmac and stone chippings down for new road surfaces. Especially in smaller communities there was always someone who was related to or friendly with an employee of the local council who worked on the local roads. Indeed, my own grandfather drove an Aveling & Porter steam road roller, and as a boy in the 1950s I used to enjoy a footplate ride when the foreman wasn't around.

Steam road rollers gave a century of service from the first recorded roller in 1865 to the mid-1960s when the last steam road roller worked in Britain. It may seem incongruous, but this Victorian invention was still good enough to roll part of Britain's first motorway, the M1. The roller was used everywhere there was a road surface: cities, towns, villages and estates all saw the roller at work. The motor roller competed on equal terms with the steam road roller for some years before the internal-combustion engine won out. This was not because the steam road rollers did a lesser job, but because like all steam engines they demanded skills and commitment to operate them and, of course, there was not the comfort or ease of maintenance afforded by the motor roller. Once the old-time drivers who usually cherished 'their' engines retired, the younger generation

of the 1950s and 1960s did not want the relative discomfort and hard, dirty work needed to keep the steam rollers running.

There are more rollers preserved and seen at steam rallies than there are any other traction engine. Many enthusiasts own a steam road roller, some actually bought out of service as being the ideal starter for ownership of a steam-powered road vehicle. These often went for reasonable prices when purchased, especially if requiring major restoration, which many did. Some local authority parks were formerly graced with redundant steam road rollers as playthings for children, but health and safety considerations have put a stop to that and most of these engines have been sold for restoration.

Like most inventions, the steam road roller had antecedents to point the way. Rollers of a kind were used in the earliest of times: history records that circular stones on a simple wooden axle and pulled by slaves or oxen were used by the Romans. They may have been primitive, but the Romans left this country with a very good road system for the time, indeed many modern roads today follow the old Roman ones. It was not until the eighteenth century that the art of road-making was rediscovered in Britain, the roads before that being really only muddy tracks in all but the major towns; early master road-builders were 'Blind Jack' Metcalfe of Yorkshire and General Wade, builder of military highways in Scotland.

The Industrial Revolution brought with it a need for better roads for the movement of goods and workers: the newly built canals offered an alternative but could not handle the increased demand for transport, and the railways were a few years hence in the nineteenth century. Turnpike Trusts were the initial answer, though these mostly improved roads on a local basis only. Then the master road-builders of the early nineteenth century, Telford and Macadam, provided a network of roads used by the stagecoach, but as the railways strengthened their grip roads began to deteriorate once again. Road repair consisted of spreading stones over the surface and allowing traffic to roll it

OPPOSITE: This 1904 Aveling & Porter road roller is taking part in a road-rolling demonstration at the Tallington Rally in May 1998. Note that the scarifier is attached ready for use behind the rear roller.

This photograph shows an Aveling & Porter 10-ton road roller actually rolling: a familiar scene repeated innumerable times across the country before the 1960s.

down which, as the authorities slowly began to recognize, was not a satisfactory solution. The middle years of the nineteenth century were therefore ripe for the invention of the steam road roller.

The steam road roller, though often considered a very British invention, in fact originated in France where rollers were trialled in the early 1860s, with massive, over 20-ton, machines fitted with horizontal boilers. The forerunner of the British steam road roller was designed by a Clark and Batho in 1863; it weighed some 30 tons and worked for a time in India. Into the picture, once again, came Thomas Aveling, who in 1862 founded with

Richard Porter the famous firm of Aveling & Porter. Three years later the firm designed and built the first of a long line of steam road rollers. The symbol of the rampant horse and the Invicta scroll, the county motto of Kent, has been proudly displayed on many thousands of rollers in many countries from that time. It is thought that two thirds of all steam road rollers sold in this country were Avelings.

Initially Aveling produced very heavy rollers of upwards of 22 tons, but because of problems encountered in use, such as hill-climbing, tonnage was scaled down until, with time and further design modifications, the 10-tonners emerged. The famous 10-tonners that can be seen at steam rallies today were available from the early 1880s, and in essence remained the same through to the end of their service 100 years later, so good was the basic design. The rollers at the front of the engine were suspended under the firebox on an upturned, U-shaped front bracket. The first engines were single-cylindered but later rollers used the compounding system, which uses steam twice (*see* Chapter 2), developed at the same time by both Aveling and the Fowler company of Leeds.

Aveling & Porter and John Fowler & Co. (Leeds) Ltd were not the only manufacturers of road rollers: with certain innovations of their own, others entered the market, especially from 1900 onwards. Notable among these were Charles Burrell & Sons Ltd who developed a single-crank compound. Many other steam works made rollers, the major ones being Wm Allchin Ltd, Armstrong-Whitworth Ltd who produced a batch in the 1920s, Clayton & Shuttleworth Ltd, Richard Garrett & Sons Ltd, Marshall, Sons & Co. Ltd, John & Henry McLaren Ltd, Robey & Co. Ltd, Ruston, Proctor & Co. Ltd, W. Tasker & Sons Ltd and Wallis & Steevens Ltd. Other factories did produce a handful of rollers, such as the Mann Patent Steam Cart & Wagon Co. Ltd, but they could not compete with the larger companies, especially Aveling, Fowler, Marshall and Wallis & Steevens, who were recognized as being the leaders in this field.

Europe produced a number of road-roller manufacturers such as Albaret, Henniger, Henschel (a well-known locomotive builder), Maffei, Ruthmeyer, the Swiss firm of SLM, and Zettelmeyer; even Skoda built a steam road roller. Our own road rollers were exported all over the world, especially to the colonies, and the basic design pioneered by Aveling and others was copied so that in some cases European rollers look very much like their British counterparts.

It is interesting to note that the internal combustion-engined roller was actually developed from the early years of the twentieth century, but because of the soundness and usability of steam, it was fifty years before diesel finally won out.

Two types of road were made by the steam road roller in its long life, waterbound and tar-based. In waterbound road-making, first the roller would use a scarifier, attached at the rear, to break up and prepare the surface. Stone brought to the roadside would be broken down by a stone crusher to a manageable size, and then be spread and watered; this was sometimes done by a horse-drawn water cart, though some rollers carried their own behind the roller. Finally the whole lot would be rolled to an even surface. Waterbound roads were not ideal as potholes appeared in the winter and dust clouds were a problem in the summer. In later years road surfaces were normally tarred and covered with chippings, in a similar manner to today's practice, and many rollers carried tar boilers behind the engine for this purpose. A contractor's road roller would very often have a living van attached, to be taken from site to site, for the driver's accommodation during the life of the contract. These vans can be seen at rallies and are very spartan, usually having just a stove, cupboards and bunks.

Convertible steam road rollers were available from some manufacturers to meet the needs of contractors who did not have all-year use for the roller: the roller could be exchanged for a set of wheels and become in effect a tractor for haulage purposes. Over the years various modifications to meet changing road-making practices were made by the manufacturers. Quick-setting tarmac required immediate rolling, for example, and some rollers were adapted accordingly. Wallis & Steevens brought out the 'Advance' type and Avelings adopted the 'Shay' principle to tandem rollers for a quick reverse, but this did not prove successful and only one example of this type survives. Also, small 5-6-tonners were built for use on sports fields, drives and footpaths.

From the mid-1920s the market slumped and this caused problems at all the steam engine manufacturers: combined with the advance of the internal-combustion engine for road haulage and other applications, the slump forced many factories to close or amalgamate. Aveling & Porter combined with other builders to form an association called Agricultural and General Engineers, and eventually formed a partnership with motor-roller manufacturers Barford & Perkins in the 1930s. This firm was called Aveling-Barford and made steam road rollers and motor rollers into the early-1950s, but this decade saw the end of production of the long-lived steam roller. So passed into history this most prolific of all road steam engines, to be born again through the efforts of the steam enthusiast, whose preservation work can be seen very often in action at road-making demonstrations at steam rallies.

Aveling & Porter

Thomas Aveling was called the 'Father of the Traction Engine' due to his pioneering work on self-propelling road steam engines. But his firm is perhaps best remembered for the ubiquitous steam road roller, the 'rampant horse' emblem on the headstock being seen all over Great Britain and abroad for almost a hundred years. The rampant horse trademark (registered in 1891) was first used in 1865, with the Latin inscription *Invicta* ('Unconquered') beneath. As his firm and farm were situated in Kent it was natural that he should use the arms of the ancient Saxon kingdom of the county.

Thomas Aveling was born at Elm, Cambridgeshire in September 1824, but moved to Rochester in Kent with his family when his mother remarried; his childhood was not a particularly happy one due to a strict clergyman stepfather. Thomas was apprenticed to a farmer, Edward Lake of Hoo St Weburgh and, having married the farmer's niece, subsequently began farming himself at Court Lodge at Ruckinge in 1850. Thomas was always more interested in the engineering side of farming than in agriculture, and at the same time he set up an agricultural-machinery repair shop in Rochester.

Thomas was always experimenting and in 1856 produced a steam plough for which he won an award. His experimentation looked towards the self-propulsion of portables, which he achieved in 1858 using a Clayton & Shuttleworth portable. Subsequent patents were taken out in 1859 and the following year, for steerage comprising at first a fifth wheel and a steersman.

Aveling made the first step towards becoming a manufacturer in 1858 when he acquired premises in High Street, Rochester, and established himself as an iron founder and agricultural engineer. Aveling also had workshops at Edwards Yard in Rochester and a foundry at Strood, on which site the famous Invicta Works was built at a later date. In the first instance his patented inventions were engineered by Clayton & Shuttleworth, but in 1861 he started building his own steam engines at Strood.

In 1862, as a result of the need for extra capital for expansion, Richard Thomas Porter joined the firm as a partner, and the famous firm of Aveling & Porter Ltd was born. Throughout the middle and late Victorian age the products of Aveling & Porter sold around the world, Australia being a particularly important market. It is interesting to note that a road locomotive in the mid-1860s cost £530, possibly £50,000 in today's prices.

Aveling & Porter diversified into all areas of agricultural equipment. Ploughing engines were especially important, though as Fowlers were the runaway leaders in this field, only three Aveling & Porter ploughing engines have been preserved. The company also produced traction engines, tractors, road locomotives, showman's road locomotive, portables and wagons, plus allied equipment – the whole spectrum of road steam.

However, its most famous product is the steam road roller, 8,600 of which were produced over the firm's life, representing two thirds of its total output. The first commercial steam road roller was produced in 1867. This was a huge roller of 30 tons which sold only in small numbers, but the 1870s saw design modifications and in the early 1880s Aveling designed a roller much as we see today, which continued in production for the following fifty years. Thomas Aveling died in March 1882 and was succeeded by his son, also Thomas (Lake) Aveling, and the firm began to expand, from employing 400 in 1872 to a thousand in 1895.

The First World War was a watershed for the company, and indeed for other manufacturers, as steam power was being replaced in many areas by the internal-combustion engine. Faced with falling orders, in 1919 Thomas Lake Aveling backed an amalgamation of several leading companies into a combine which, it was hoped, would alleviate their collective problems and combat competition. The new company was called Agricultural and General Engineers Ltd and included Barford & Perkins, Blackstone, Burrell, Garrett, Davey Paxman, J.F. Howard and others. The constituent firms still produced engines and allied equipment under their own brands, so Aveling & Porter continued as a marque. The 1920s saw the end of production of Aveling's ploughing engines and steam wagons.

The early 1930s saw financial problems for Agricultural and General Engineers Ltd and the firm collapsed in 1932. However, from the ashes rose the new firm of Aveling-Barford Ltd to manufacture steam and motor rollers. At the time this new firm was the world's largest manufacturer of road rollers, and it continued until recent times.

Of the 12,200 steam-powered vehicles produced by the firm there are nearly 600 examples preserved, and of these 75 per cent are steam road rollers – a fitting tribute to this very fine engineering firm.

The 1894 Aveling & Porter 10-ton road roller 'Sarah' is seen at the road-making demonstration area at the June 2003 Banbury Rally.

A 1901 Aveling & Porter road roller at Walk Farm, Chipping Norton, at a Society of Enginemen's road run in November 2000. This roller originally worked for Oxfordshire County Council.

TOP LEFT: *This is the sole surviving example of the nine vertical twin-cylinder, shay-geared roller type (2RR) built by Aveling & Porter. This example from 1911, named 'Chimaera', is seen at the Rushmoor Rally in May 1998.*

TOP RIGHT: *A big 15-tonner on a road run in October 2003 at Little Chalfont in the Chilterns, with the autumn colours behind; this is the 1916 Aveling & Porter 'Jupiter'.*

BELOW: *The 1920 Aveling & Porter 10-ton road roller 'Major' at rest in Inkberrow village, Worcestershire on a local road run.*

A 1923 Aveling & Porter 10-ton road roller causes a classic traffic jam as she runs through Castle Combe in May 1993, followed by a Bristol Bus.

BELOW LEFT: 'Churchill', a 10-ton Aveling & Porter road roller built in 1923, on the demonstration working area at the Stoke Row Rally in June 2000.

BELOW RIGHT: A 1923 Aveling & Porter 10-ton road roller is seen on the road near Hanbury, Worcestershire in September 2002, with cart and living van in tow.

TOP LEFT: *The 1926 Aveling & Porter 8-ton road roller 'Viatect', on a road run in Gloucestershire, nears Haw Bridge on the B4213, complete with cart and living van.*

TOP RIGHT: *The 1932 Aveling & Porter 6-ton road roller 'Daisy' is captured on the road at Alcester Heath, Warwickshire in September 1992.*

The successor to Aveling & Porter was Aveling-Barford, at one time the largest manufacturer of rollers of all kinds in the world. Here the 1937-built 10-tonner named 'Patricia' is seen on a road run at Welford on Avon, Warwickshire in 2003.

A 1912 Clayton & Shuttleworth 10-ton road roller standing outside the imposing Walcot Hall in Shropshire at the 1991 Bishops Castle Rally.

The 1912-built 12½-ton Burrell road roller 'Jeanette' at the Weeting Rally in July 1999.

The 1926 Burrell 10-ton road roller 'Heather' on the road approaching the rally site at Roxton in September 1993.

A 1921 Fowler 10-ton road roller with living van entering the Fromebridge Inn grounds in Gloucestershire, on a road run organized by the local Stroud Vintage Transport and Engine Club.

The road roller illustrated above right pictured at night at the 2004 Kemble Rally.

A re-creation scene from the 1930s using the 1922 Fowler 10-ton road roller 'Busy Bee', a former Oxfordshire County Council roller. She is seen here scarifying at Cholsey, near Reading.

ABOVE: *A 12-ton Fowler road roller built in 1930, named 'Arfur', heads a line-up of engines resting after a road run at Chenies village in the Chilterns. Behind is a Burrell traction engine and an Aveling & Porter road roller.*

Another view of the re-creation scene from the 1930s. Here the crew are posing around the engine, dressed appropriately and carrying the tools of the road-making trade. This re-creation was inspired by some photographs from the 1930s discovered by the owner, the late Ran Hawthorne, who set up this scene to replicate what the photos showed. Behind the engine is the former Great Western Railway main line, near Cholsey Station.

A 1937 Fowler 8-ton road roller on a road run with a living van at Charlecote Park, near Stratford upon Avon, in August 1998.

BELOW LEFT: *A rare engine: 'Rosie' is an 8-ton road roller, built in 1917 by the Leeds firm of T. Green & Sons, only five of whose engines are preserved. She is seen here at Govers Hill, Porthowen, Cornwall at the July 1995 West of England Steam Engine Society road run.*

BELOW RIGHT: *The earliest known Garrett road roller, a 10-tonner built in 1910 and named 'Elizabeth', at Yoxley on the occasion of the East Anglian Traction Engine Club's road run in May 1997.*

D.C. KNIGHT. TRELILL. BODMIN.

FJB 990

A very late-built (1943) 12-ton Marshall road roller at Engine Hill, Porthowen, Cornwall at the July 1995 West of England Steam Engine Society road run.

NR 6120

J.J. CRANE Wolverhampton

The 1925-built 10-ton Marshall road roller 'Jane' at Astwood Bank, Worcestershire in September 1994.

Robey & Co. Ltd

This firm was founded by Robert Robey in 1854 at Perseverance Works (later the Globe Works), Canwick Road, Lincoln. The first traction engine was built in 1861 and exhibited at the Great Exhibition in 1862, portable engines having been produced from the very beginning of the firm.

Robey collaborated with an Edinburgh man called Thomson in the late 1860s to build the very unusual Thomson Road Steamer, though other firms were also involved. The power was provided by a vertical boiler and duplex cylinders, transmitted by two-speed gearing. There were Thomson patent rubber tyres on the driving wheels and a steel-shod steering wheel, and the engine worked with an omnibus body.

Robey built railway locomotives in both narrow and standard gauge. Like many other firms, besides portables, they built stationary engines for use in factories: these came in both vertical and horizontal boiler forms, and included single, duplex, compound and expansion versions.

The Robey traction engine was subject to much development work from its inception in 1861 and the final versions in the late nineteenth and early twentieth century were of a high standard, available in single or compound engines of various ratings. Like many other firms, Robey took advantage of the 1904 Orders and built a 5-ton steam tractor of businesslike appearance.

Robey produced steam road rollers from 1910 onwards, and in particular developed and built the 'Tandem' roller and, in the 1920s, the 'Tri-Tandem' roller which used the quick-reverse principle for rolling where speed was essential. Robey also produced a steam wagon of overtype design in the 1920s using a similar power unit to the tandem roller, with three speeds and final drive by chain.

Around sixty examples have been preserved, a mix of portables, traction engines, tractors, road rollers and wagons.

A 1925 7½-ton Robey road roller, an example of the tandem-roller type, at the Lincolnshire Rally in 2002.

The 1930-built Robey tri-tandem road roller 'Herts Wanderer' at the St Austell Rally, Cornwall in 1998; only two of these unusual rollers still exist.

The 1911 Ruston & Hornsby 11-ton road roller 'Bransford Bear' on a road run in Gloucestershire at Haw Bridge.

The very last built and preserved Wallis & Steevens 'Advance', a 1939 8-ton road roller, is shown here at the Great Dorset Steam Fair in September 2003.

A re-creation of the road-making scenes once seen all over the country, with a Wallis & Steevens 'Advance' road roller, an Aveling & Porter road roller, the living van, a coal supply and the foreman's Austin Seven car in the foreground. This was set up at the Tallington Rally in May 1992.

Chapter 4
Steam Wagons and Cars

STEAM WAGONS arrived late on the steam traction scene and remained in operation for only around fifty years. Only two manufacturers carried the flag for this type of road steam beyond the mid-1920s with any distinction, these being the well-known firms of Fodens and Sentinel. It is interesting to note that most builders, including Fodens, called their product 'wagons', but Sentinel always referred to their products as 'waggons'. (In this book 'wagon' is used except where the text refers to Sentinels.)

Various factors inhibited the growth of wagons on the roads, firstly the notorious 1865 'Red Flag' Act, which required all mechanically propelled vehicles to have a man walking in front with a red flag to warn of its approach. The red flag part of the Act was rescinded in 1876, but this very restrictive Act was only fully repealed in 1896, by the Locomotive Act; up to that time, therefore, the development of road transportation for both freight and passenger transport was heavily restricted. Also, the major steam manufacturers produced the traction engine and the smaller tractor for haulage, which for the prevailing conditions of the age were considered satisfactory.

As related in the previous chapter, Great Britain's roads were not in good condition in large areas of the country: waterbound roads caused dust clouds in the summer and broke up in the winter, and tarmacadamed roads were slow to appear. Of course, road conditions were not helped by the major means of road transportation in the late nineteenth century – the horse, cart and wagon – whose passing often left difficult road surfaces for mechanized transport. The other major factor was the railways, which enjoyed rapid expansion in the second half of the nineteenth century. The railway companies enjoyed a virtual monopoly in the long-distance carriage of freight and people,

with branch lines to cater for short trips. In those days many industrial concerns had railway lines built into their works so that goods could be immediately despatched around the country – some say we ought to return to those days now! Against the backdrop of all these factors the growth of steam, and indeed the later internal combustion-engined road transport, was much restricted.

We have seen in previous chapters how traction engines became self propelled and various types were manufactured for haulage purposes. However, the principle of a chassis to carry goods integrated to the engine was slow to evolve. The move towards the steam wagon was gradual, tentative beginnings being made from the 1870s onwards, early wagons being built mainly on locomotive principles. In 1870 a 'wagon' was produced by a John Yale of Glasgow, then in 1875 the well-known Devizes traction engine company, Brown & May, also produced a 'wagon'. The next recorded prototype is said to have been from James Sumner of Leyland in 1884. The following years up to the late 1890s saw a few more firms testing the water, but none were mass produced.

While goods could be and were moved around the country by traction engines with trailers, and agricultural machinery between contract locations, these were slow and cumbersome. The roads of the day were not designed for this very heavy and wide form of transport, especially in the countryside where often narrow, unsurfaced lanes linked villages. The steam wagon, while initially based on the traction engine, moved away from that form of design toward the modern style of wagon or lorry. These characteristics were: an identifiable cab at the front instead of a footplate at the rear; a load-carrying base built as an integral part of the chassis; and, above all, road wheels similar to those used today – if loosely based, in the case of early wagons, on scaled-down traction-engine wheels. Trailers could still be used, but were not essential for haulage tasks as they were with the traction engine.

OPPOSITE: A 1920-built Clayton & Shuttleworth 5-ton wagon at the Great Dorset Steam Fair in September 1994.

A superb working-environment picture of the now-preserved 1928 6nhp Foden wagon (works no. 13196) 'Pride of Fulham', in its days with the London coal firm Camroux, probably soon after the Second World War.

The steam wagon was built in two types, overtype and undertype. Overtype wagons had a horizontal boiler with the engine above the boiler, as in traction engines; undertypes comprised a vertical boiler with the engine below the chassis. To complicate matters there were variations on the undertype theme – some had a horizontal boiler, but all had the engine below the chassis.

It was at the turn of the twentieth century that a range of wagons became available to the commercial haulage contractor. These were built in the main by traction-engine manufacturers, though new builders also entered the market. Some of these manufacturers were well-known: Wm. Allchin of Northampton; Aveling & Porter of Rochester; Alley & McLellan Ltd of Polmadie, better known as Sentinel Waggon Works and eventually relocating to Shrewsbury; Charles Burrell, Sons

& Co. of Thetford; Clayton Wagons of Lincoln; Edwin Foden, Son & Co. Ltd of Sandbach; Wm. Foster & Co. of Lincoln; John Fowler & Co. Ltd of Leeds; Richard Garrett & Co. Ltd of Leiston; Leyland (Lancashire Steam Works) & Co. of Leyland; Mann's Patent Steam Cart & Wagon Co. of Leeds; Thorneycroft Steam Wagon Co. of Basingstoke; Wantage Engineering Co. of Wantage; and Yorkshire Patent Steam Wagon Co. of Leeds.

Some lesser-known makes who only built in the period up to the First World War were English Steam Wagon Co. of Hebden Bridge; E. S. Hindley & Sons of Bourton; Lifu (Liquid Fuel Engineering Co.) of Cowes; C. and A. Musker of Liverpool; St Pancras Ironworks Co. Ltd of London; Straker Steam Vehicle Co. of London; and Thames Engineering Works of Greenwich. In all, a staggering ninety or so manufacturers built steam wagons in this country. However, only a handful of these survived beyond 1930: Allchin, Fodens, Garrett, Robey, Sentinel and Yorkshire. None survived as steam wagon manufacturers beyond the beginning of the Second World War. Fodens and Sentinel went on to build diesel versions of their wagons and, improbable as it may seem, Sentinel received an order in 1949 to build a batch of 100 steamers for use in Argentina at the Rio Turbio coal mines. These were used to carry coal to the coast prior to the building of a railway line, which when built in 1955 itself operated steam locomotives; it is known that one or two of these waggons survive in South America.

While the steam wagon is generally considered a British invention, they were built in reasonable numbers in Europe and America. Hanomag of Germany was a well-known steam manufacturer, as was the Swiss firm of SLM (which also built distinctive road rollers). Sentinel-designed waggons were built by Skoda, and Garrett had a similar arrangement with Adamov Engineering Works, like Skoda from Czechoslovakia, and the locomotive builder Henschel also produced some. Details are sketchy, but some examples of these foreign makes exist in preservation. America was the home of the steam car (*see* below) and it was to be expected that steam wagons would be built. As in Britain, a number of traction-engine builders diversified into this field, and it is recorded that there were thirty-one wagon makers in the USA. These included: Buffalo-Springfield of Springfield, Ohio; Doble Steam Motor Company of Emeryville, California; Michigan Steam Motor Co.; Stanley Motor Carriage Co. of Newton, Massachusetts; and White Motor Co. of Cleveland, Ohio.

Though the last steam wagons were built in the late 1930s, haulage contractors kept using the vehicles into the late 1950s in some cases, many, of course, being treasured for what they were. It is amazing that the steam wagon carried on as long as it did considering the competition from the petrol and diesel lorries, which had the advantages of more comfortable cabs, relative ease of starting, no messy preparation, no handling dirty coal, no stops for water and no commitment required to keep steam working.

Because of their relatively late working life a number of wagons survived into the period of active preservation, and that is why the two most prolific manufacturers, Fodens and Sentinel, are well represented. Each firm built around 6,500 wagons and tractors, of which over eighty Fodens and nearly 120 Sentinels exist in preservation and are a regular sight at steam rallies. Of the other manufacturers only a handful exist from makers such as Aveling & Porter, Clayton & Shuttleworth, Foster, Garrett, Leyland, Mann, Ransomes, Sims & Jefferies, Robey, Tasker,

Thorneycroft, Wallis & Steevens and Yorkshire. Some makes, however, are lost for ever, unless they remain undiscovered in some remote location, including Allchin, Burrell, Coulthard, Savage and Straker.

Following on from wagons, a close cousin is that most delightful of steam-powered vehicles, the steam car. This is not really a traction engine but it shares the most important part of a steam engine, the boiler. Though the steam car is very similar to the steam wagon its heyday was even shorter, approximately from 1900 to the mid-1920s. The USA was the home of the steam car: there were almost 125 makes in America, and though they were built in other countries, including Great Britain, production did not approach the same scale as that of the USA. All steam cars work on more or less the same principle. The boilers are of strong, lightweight construction but work at high pressure and are fired from a burner fuelled by kerosene (paraffin) or modern diesel or petrol fuel.

Stanley steamers, built at Newton, Massachusetts, are the most well-known steam cars, and are occasionally seen at rallies. Other manufacturers were White from Cleveland, the well-known Doble from Detroit, and the Locomobile from Bridgeport, Connecticut, who bought out Stanley in the 1920s. While the heyday of the steam car was the first two decades of the twentieth century, companies like Doble continued throughout the 1930s and 1940s; steam car engines also powered speedboats and railcars, and were even tried in an aeroplane in the 1950s. Two makes built in Great Britain and preserved are the Morris of London and the Turner Miesse which, despite its name, was built in Wolverhampton from 1903–12 under licence from Miesse et Cie of Belgium.

These veterans do motor on and in the case of those built around the First World War and early 1920s can quite easily keep up with modern traffic, with speeds of up to 60mph (100km/h) – these steam cars must have been about the fastest road vehicles that money could buy in the first two decades of the twentieth century. Some of the selling points in contemporary advertisements state that steam cars set performance goals such as smooth and rapid acceleration, simplicity of power control and maximum torque at zero speed. It was some time before the automotive industry could approach the standards set by the steamers. In January, 1906, at Ormond Beach, Florida, a Stanley Steamer driven by one Fred Marriott became the fastest car in the world at a staggering average speed of 127.66mph (205.4km/h); a year later this car reached 190mph (306km/h) before being destroyed in an accident. Apparently a replica is being built in the USA to appear at the centenary of the event.

TOP LEFT: *The rare Aveling & Porter wagon: this example, built in 1922 and named 'Lady Fiona', is a 5-tonner imported from Australia, hence the livery. It is seen here at the Great Dorset Steam Fair in September 1994.*

TOP RIGHT: *A 1920-built Clayton & Shuttleworth 5-ton wagon named 'Fenland Princess', at the Leighton Buzzard Rally in May 2004.*

A 1912 Foden 3-ton wagon standing next to the 1902 Hovis/Ford Light Steam Delivery Baker's Van, seen at the Kemble Rally in July 2003. The baker's van was rebuilt in 1972–73 from a Ford body of 1902 and a locomobile steam car engine of 1900; this vehicle can cruise at 20mph (30km/h).

Fodens Ltd

Fodens are well known in the steam world for their wagons, and in their day were the great rivals of Sentinel. These two makes carried the flag for road steam power against the internal-combustion engine up to and – in a limited way – beyond the Second World War. However, Fodens were much more than producers of steam wagons: they also built some fine agricultural traction engines, road locomotives and showman's engines, though the firm did not venture into production of portables or road rollers.

The firm can be traced back to 1856 as Hancock & Foden, builders of agricultural machinery, and eventually in 1882 the first traction engine was produced. Edwin Foden (1841–1911) was the founder and the works was situated at Sandbach, Cheshire: this was an unusual location for a traction-engine company, as most firms were either in East Anglia, Yorkshire, Hampshire or Kent. Sandbach remained the home of this firm in its various guises until the 1990s.

The first steam wagon was produced in 1901, after two years of experimentation. A year later, coinciding with the firm's title becoming Fodens Ltd, the 5-ton wagon was made; 3- and 4-ton versions were also built, this type continuing in production until 1923. The engine was an overtype with a horizontal boiler, the driver sitting behind the boiler with cylinders and engine mounted above in the style of a traction engine. During the First World War steam wagons were used for carrying supplies to the troops, Fodens being particularly favoured for this work.

In 1920 the C-type 5/6-tonners was produced. These were a much improved design including a full-width cab, though they still used the overtype layout. Due to competition from firms like Sentinel, Fodens only produced undertype models in the late 1920s (four and six wheelers called the 'E' type), and the model 'S6'.

Tractors, which Fodens built in large numbers, were in effect cut-down wagons and were particularly useful in the timber industry and for haulage use with differing types of trailers. These tractors were also occasionally used by showmen; these were fitted with dynamos and were decorated with the barley-twist canopy supports and brilliant liveries favoured by the fairground operators. One Foden had an omnibus body fitted to carry the Foden Works Band, and a replica of this vehicle has been built and can be seen at rallies in the deep brown livery of the company.

Competition from the internal-combustion engine and punitive taxation on road steam saw the final steam wagon built by Fodens in 1934. By that time some 6,500 examples had left the factory, coincidentally virtually the same number as produced by their great rivals, Sentinel.

In 1930 Fodens moved into the production of diesel lorries, and the company split in 1932, Edwin Richard Foden founding ERF. The company was taken over by the American Paccor Company in 1980 and the Fodens brand name continued, though vehicle production moved in 1999 to Leyland in Lancashire.

Around ninety Foden wagons and tractors survive, but as the firm was not a high-volume producer of traction engines only a handful of other types – less than twenty – remain.

A 1926 Foden tractor at Castle Combe in May 2002.

This 1928 Foden 6-wheel, 12-ton model K3 is the only one of its type and is seen at the Weeting Rally in 1998.

BELOW LEFT: The 1924 Foden 6-ton wagon, named 'Pride of Somerset/Freddie', is captured at the 2002 Welland Rally.

BELOW RIGHT: The 1914 Foden steam bus 'Irene' at the Marcle Rally in 2002. This was built as a wagon, bought in a derelict state in 2000 and restored with a replica of the Foden Works Band bus body.

A 1932 8-ton Foden tractor at Horsehay, Shropshire. This wagon was originally used for timber haulage in the local area.

BELOW LEFT: A 1930 6-ton Foden wagon on a road run near Gamlingay in Bedfordshire.

BELOW RIGHT: The 1931 5-ton Foden wagon 'Lady Catherine' at Ditton Priors, Shropshire. First registered as a 3-way tipper by Derbyshire County Council and eventually converted to a tar-sprayer, this wagon became a water tanker in 1962, eventually having the current furniture body fitted in preservation.

A 1916 6-ton Sentinel Super Waggon seen on a road run, passing an unusual cricket pavilion at Heyshott Green, Surrey in July 1995.

BELOW LEFT: *The only preserved wagon built by Ransomes, Sims & Jefferies, a 5-ton version from 1923. This has been imported from Australia and rebuilt in Great Britain, and is pictured at the June 2003 Banbury Rally.*

BELOW RIGHT: *A 1925 6-ton Robey wagon pictured at the Great Dorset Steam Fair in September 1994.*

A six-wheeler Sentinel DG6 waggon, built in 1930 and named 'Shrewsbury Knight', is followed into the site of Roxton Rally by a 1924 Sentinel Super Waggon in September 1993.

Steam road and rail meet, narrow-gauge style, at the Castle Caerenion Station on the Welshpool and Llanfair Railway. Beyer, Peacock no. 823, 'The Countess' standing next to a 1929 Sentinel DG4 tar-spraying waggon in November 2004.

TOP LEFT: *The 1931 Sentinel DG4 Waggon of Morris's Lubricants stands next to a 1928 Ford Model AA van, also in Morris's Lubricants livery, outside the Canal Tavern in Shrewsbury, across the road from the Works. The waggon was built for Samuel Barber & Co. of Bootle, then worked for Paul Brothers, millers of Birkenhead, and was bought for preservation in 1949. The Sentinel Waggon Works was located in Shrewsbury near the Morris Oils firm, and the two firms collaborated to produce steam oils.*

TOP RIGHT: *A 1935 Sentinel S4 Waggon seen at the approaches to Stanway Hall, Gloucestershire in October 2001.*

BELOW: *Three types of Sentinel waggon, all built in 1934, are displayed here at the Woodcote Rally in July 2003. From left to right, an S4, an S6 and an S8 (wheel configurations).*

Sentinel Waggon Works Ltd

The roots of the Sentinel are in Scotland and the story of this famous waggon works starts in the 1870s when the founders of the original company, Stephen Alley and John Maclellan, both engineers, started the firm of Alley & Maclellan in London Road, Glasgow. (Sentinel always referred to their products as 'waggons' rather than 'wagons', and this usage is continued when discussing Sentinel products here.) In 1880 the engineering firm moved to new premises named 'The Sentinel Works' at Polmadie, Glasgow.

The firm originally made valves, but in 1885 they started building the very successful 'Sentinel High Speed Steam Engine'. This engine had several applications: the generation of electricity, marine craft propulsion and powering factory machinery. The firm also built water-borne craft, launches, barges and some larger vehicles in their own shipyard at Polmadie.

As with many other traction engine companies, the Heavy Motor Car Order 1904 convinced Alley & Maclellan that they should enter the market for steam waggons. In 1903, while development work was carried out at Alley & Maclellans the firm took over the manufacturing rights of an early steam lorry developed in Horsehay, Shropshire called the Simpson-Bibby after the inventor Daniel Simpson. Further development in Glasgow resulted in the so-called 'Standard' Sentinel of 1905; these were originally named the model 5-ton tipper, model 6-ton flat, and so on, the 'Standard' title coming into use at a later date. The boiler used in the 'Standard' was designed by Stephen Alley and was such a good design that it remained in use, with modifications, until the demise of the Sentinel steam waggon in the early 1950s. Before the First World War Sentinel produced both undertype, which they favoured, and overtype models. These cost between £600–660, dependent on specification.

Sales increased during the war, and Alley & Maclellan decided that a new factory was required to concentrate solely on steam waggons. In 1915 the famous 'Sentinel Waggon Works' was built on the Whitchurch Road on the outskirts of Shrewsbury and all production of steam waggons was concentrated there, some skilled men transferring from Glasgow to Shrewsbury. Sentinel also constructed a housing estate for its workers on the Whitchurch Road, near the factory, the firm often using it as the backdrop for official works photographs of their waggons. Stephen Alley sold his shares in Alley & Maclellan to Beardmores in 1918 and purchased the Shrewsbury Works; the Glasgow factory now leaves the Sentinel story.

'Standard' Sentinel steam waggons were made up to 1923, when a new model, the 'Super', was introduced. This was fitted with a single gear; it was built in the form of waggons, tractors, rail locomotives, railcars and stationary engines. In the late 1920s the double-geared DG was produced, in four- and six-wheel variations, the models DG4 and DG6; the rigid-six version became very popular with hauliers. The final version of the DG models was the impressive DG8, being built to carry 15 tons in weight and 29ft (8.8m) long. The DG4 had a payload of 6 to 7 tons, the DG6 and DG8 of 12 tons. (The DG8 carried a similar payload to the DG6 due to prevailing legal weight limits.)

The 'S' models came out in 1932; these were lighter machines than the DG range, with optional modern rotating fire grates, automatic stoking and a shaft drive replacing the chain drive. These models came in four-, six- and eight-wheeled versions. Due to competition from the internal combustion engine, this final series was phased out in the late 1930s; however, the final order for steam waggons, from Argentina, was actually built in 1950.

The company had experimented with diesel lorries in the 1930s, and after the Second World War, in 1948, production began of a new range of four- and six-wheel diesel lorries, powered by Sentinel's own 4-cylinder engine. Sales of these lorries reduced in the 1950s to such an extent that production ceased in 1956 and the Sentinel Waggon Works was bought by Rolls-Royce for diesel-engine production. The Sentinel diesel lorry was manufactured by a new company, Transport Vehicles (Warrington), set up in 1957, but this venture only lasted until 1961, and ceased trading in that year.

Around 120 of all types of Sentinel steam waggons and tractors have been preserved, from a 'Standard' of 1914 to a 1938 S4, though some specials have been constructed. Also preserved are examples of the steam rail locomotives, usually shunters, and a Sentinel railcar actually works on special occasions in Sri Lanka.

The 1934 Sentinel DG4 waggon 'Proctors Pride' at the Great Dorset Steam Fair in September 2004. This waggon was new to and one of a pair sold to Brown & Sons of Chelmsford, Essex, and used commercially until 1956.

Two rare makes of wagon seen together at the July 1993 Downs Rally: a 1924 5-ton Tasker wagon and, nearest the camera, a 1912 Wallis & Steevens 5-ton wagon. Both are normally kept in museums.

A 5-ton Thornycroft wagon from 1900 is pictured at the Great Dorset Steam Fair in September 1994 It is one of only three preserved.

A wagon line-up at the 2004 Kemble Rally with four makes represented: Ransome, Sims & Jefferies, Foden, Sentinel and Yorkshire.

A 1905 2-ton Yorkshire, named 'Denby Maiden', seen here at the August 2002 Lincolnshire Rally.

LEFT: *A 1906 Morriss steam car, built in London, standing next to the signal box at Highley Station on the Severn Valley Railway during the Steam Car Club of Great Britain's annual outing in July 2003.*

BELOW: *The 1927 6-ton Yorkshire wagon 'Yorkshire Lad' at the Kemble Rally in August 2004. It was built new for Clayton of Hunslet, Leeds and rebuilt at the works in 1936.*

A line-up of Stanley steam cars each side of the 1923-built (so younger than the cars) Vale of Rheidol Railway no. 8, a 2-6-2T steam locomotive. The venue is Devils Bridge Station, at the Steam Car Club of Great Britain's annual outing to Wales in July 2004.

The impressive 1910 Stanley Model 85 with the signalman looking on, outside Bridgnorth Station signal box on the Severn Valley Railway, during the Steam Car Club of Great Britain's annual outing in July 2003.

Chapter 5
Ploughing Engines

WHEN one looks at the history of the ploughing engine there really is only one name and one builder, and that is John Fowler and his Leeds firm of John Fowler & Co. Ltd, the Steam Plough Works.

One of the most interesting sights at a steam rally is the working area, especially if steam cultivation is being demonstrated. While engines for threshing, stone crushing and sawing all have their devotees, the sheer presence of a pair of Fowler ploughing engine stands out. These giants of agriculture are an impressive sight when they take up a working implement, the driver opens the regulator and the engine emits the familiar bark of a Fowler going to work at ploughing, dredging or harrowing. The ploughing engine and the various methods employed to prepare fields for planting have been around since the 1850s, which is basically as long as the traction engine has been working in agriculture. The four systems used were the 'roundabout' system, the single-engine system, the double-engine system and the direct-traction system.

The roundabout system was carried out by a portable engine or traction engine. A wire rope would be attached to a windlass and an implement – such as plough or harrow – would be pulled backwards and forwards. This wire was carried around the field by a system of pulleys that were moved around the field until the work was complete. This method is occasionally demonstrated at steam rallies.

The single-engine system used a single engine, usually a portable, placed in a prominent position in the field to be worked. A drum of wire rope was attached to the engine and a self-moving anchor was positioned at the other end of the field.

The rope was played out from the drum and around the anchor, carrying the implement back and forth.

The double-engine system was the best known and most widely used method of steam cultivation, and is the one usually demonstrated at steam rallies. The engines were positioned at either end of the field, each with a drum to wind the rope to which the implement was attached, which passed back and forth between them. The engine not working would edge forward one length as the other pulled the plough or cultivator; once it had reached the end the whistle would sound, the implement was turned and the cycle repeated.

Direct-traction cultivation, as the name implies, involved the traction engine pulling (or pushing) the implement across the field, as a modern tractor does today. However, the weight of a traction engine caused problems with soil compaction and if conditions were wet it could sink. It was not widely used in Great Britain, but in North America direct ploughing was practised extensively. The Mann traction engine company actually advertised their light steam tractors as being suitable for direct ploughing at the turn of the twentieth century, but whether the advertising was successful is in doubt. This type of cultivation is occasionally demonstrated at rallies, if conditions allow.

The cultivation of the land, the need to till the soil, to grow crops and to harvest, has been one of man's concerns since the dawn of history. For thousands of years this was done by hand or with the help of oxen or horse, and even up to and beyond the age of steam this was the preferred way to cultivate the land.

A succession of ideas for harnessing the power of steam to serve agriculture was promoted from the start of the nineteenth century, some just on paper, some actually designed and built. Steam diggers were a favourite and a number were built and successfully used. In the 1830s much work was carried out on land drainage by steam, using a primitive version of the roundabout system. A prototype was built and tested by

The early 1873-built 14nhp Fowler ploughing engine 'Noreen', seen here with the plough at rest. This engine has been rebuilt with an Allen boiler.

An 1876-built Fowler 8nhp ploughing engine getting ready to work at the July 1996 Weeting Rally.

The 1916 12nhp Fowler K7 ploughing engine 'Linkey' about to start work at the 2004 Welland Rally.

The 1916 10nhp Fowler T1 ploughing engine 'Master John' pulling a harrow at the Waddesdon Rally in September 1991.

BELOW LEFT: The 1918 16nhp Fowler BB1 ploughing engine 'Headland Beauty' climbs Engine Hill, Porthowen, Cornwall at the West of England Steam Engine Society's road run in July 1995.

BELOW RIGHT: A 1918 16nhp Fowler BB1 ploughing engine speeds along the road from Hanbury to Feckenham, Worcestershire in September 1997.

John Fowler & Co.

John Fowler & Co. were responsible for the majority of the mighty steam ploughing engines that revolutionized agriculture in mid-Victorian times. Other manufacturers built these engines but Fowler was far and away the most prolific, and this is evidenced by the numbers in preservation. Fowler's were, however, much more than builders of ploughing engines. Besides fine traction engines they were also renowned for road locomotives and showman's engines, and their road rollers vied with Avelings for a time in popular use.

John Fowler was born in Melksham, Wiltshire on 11 July 1826, to a wealthy Quaker merchant family. By the age of twenty-one he had joined the Middlesborough engineering firm of Gilkes, Wilson, Hopkins & Co., locomotive and mining engineers. A visit to Ireland where he saw great poverty convinced him that he could assist by mechanizing agriculture. Initially Fowler concentrated on land drainage, as he had seen the extensive bogs and marshes in Ireland, and in 1854 he had perfected a steam-driven method of land drainage, using a portable. It was a short step from there for Fowler to perfect actual ploughing by steam, and in 1857 the first self-moving ploughing engines were constructed for the inventor by Clayton & Shuttleworth.

John Fowler was aided in his experiments by associates such as Fry, Worby, Head, Burton and especially David Greig, a Scottish farmer who eventually became a partner in the firm. Also Fowler was fortunate in engaging the top engineering firms of the day, Clayton & Shuttleworth, Ransomes & Sims, Robert Stephenson & Co. and Kitson, Thompson & Hewitson to build his engines and agricultural equipment.

In 1862 John Fowler established himself in his own Steam Plough Works in Leeds, where all manufacturing was carried out. John Fowler's brother Robert became a partner in 1864, but tragedy struck at the end of the year when John Fowler died at the early age of thirty-eight in a hunting accident.

The firm was established with good orders by then and John Fowler's partners carried on the innovative work started by him. Almost immediately traction engines and portables were added to the portfolio and the following decades saw much experimentation to improve all types of engine. In the early-1880s compounding (the re-use of steam) was introduced to traction engines. Due to an excellent reputation for workmanship and finish, Fowler steam engines sold well, both at home and abroad.

The firm branched out in the last two decades of the nineteenth century to build steam road rollers, stationary engines, narrow-gauge railway locomotives, colliery equipment and electricity-generating plant. During this time the Fowler steam ploughing engines and dedicated tackle sold all over the world, into the first decades of the twentieth century.

As for most steam engineering firms, the First World War and its aftermath caused great problems for Fowler as the glut of second-hand machinery from the war and the march of the internal-combustion engine took its toll. Fowler's weathered the period better than most, turning out their products for a steady and loyal market in road and showman's locomotives, as well as ploughing engines and agricultural equipment. The mid-1920s saw Fowler bring out a steam wagon, developed during the war, which in a small way was successful in platform and tipping versions. They also made a gully emptier, to clear drains, for local authorities.

The firm not only exported but also established a number of overseas subsidiaries, especially in Europe, where engines were built under licence, and proved very profitable for Fowler's especially just prior to the First World War.

However, the 1930 legislation (changes to road taxation) that discriminated against road steam virtually finished production, only a handful being built up to 1937 when the last Fowler steam engine, a road roller, was sold. With one last fling the factory turned out six 'Super Lion' showman's engines; the last of these, built in 1934 and called 'Supreme', is now preserved and a fitting tribute to the very fine steam engines produced by this prolific factory.

The firm was eventually absorbed in 1947 into the T. W. Ward Group and Fowler's were no more. Nearly 700 examples of this make have been preserved, more than any other make, of which ploughing engines account for 25 per cent of the total.

A 1918 16nhp Fowler BB1 ploughing engine stands awaiting work with its harrow at the Steam Plough Club's annual meeting at Avon Dassett, Warwickshire in July 2002.

The 1918 18nhp Fowler AA7 ploughing engine
'Repulse' doing its turn of duty with the plough at
the Steam Plough Club's annual meeting at Avon
Dassett, Warwickshire in July 2002.

A 1916 12nhp Fowler K7 ploughing engine pulling a
harrow at the July 2000 Welland Rally, with the
Malvern Hills in the background.

A 1919 16nhp Fowler BB1 ploughing engine pulls the plough towards it at the Great Ploughing Challenge at Boddington, Oxfordshire in 2003.

The 1925 14nhp Fowler BB1 ploughing engine 'Bonzor Tom' awaits a turn of duty with the harrow at the July 1999 Weeting Rally.

At the July 2002 Weeting Rally the 1925 the 16nhp Fowler BB1 ploughing engine 'Saucy Sue' gets ready to pull a harrow.

One of the awesome 22nhp Fowler Z7 ploughing engines, in this case a 1922 version, receives the plough at the Steam Plough Club's annual meeting in July 2002 at Avon Dassett, Warwickshire.

The 1925 16nhp Fowler K7 ploughing engine 'John' at the National Vintage Tractor Engine Club's Rally in South Croxton, Leicestershire in August 2000. This engine, one of a pair, is resident at the Lincolnshire Museum of Rural Life.

ABOVE: *A Fowler BB1 ploughing engine working for real, dredging a lake at a farm at Shobden, Herefordshire in 2003.*

One of the mighty 22nhp Fowler Z7 ploughing engines of 1922 passes a plough at the September 1992 Waddesdon Rally.

ABOVE: Road meets rail steam at the October 1998 Gloucestershire Warwickshire Railway Steam Rally at Toddington Station. 'Jinty' 47383 and Great Western Railway 6960 'Ravening ham Hall' look over the fields to a 1918 16nhp Fowler BB1 ploughing engine and the plough.

LEFT: The unique J. & F. Howard ploughing engine named 'The Farmer's Engine', thought to be 1870s built, at the Great Ploughing Challenge at Boddington, Oxfordshire in 2003.

BELOW: Dating from 1918, the only preserved 14nhp (there is also a 22nhp version) McLaren ploughing engine, named 'Avis', at work with the plough at the Great Ploughing Challenge at Boddington, Oxfordshire in 2003.

A 1918 Fowler BB1 converted to diesel power, seen at the Great Dorset Steam Fair in September 1999.

TOP RIGHT: *The 1926 Wilder 12nhp ploughing engine 'No. 1 William' was built in that year using components of early Fowler ploughing engines (from 1869), and boiler and cylinder blocks built by Wilders. This engine worked from 1927 to 1933 and again in the late 1940s before entering preservation.*

RIGHT: *Direct ploughing, never very successful in this country, is demonstrated by the 5-ton 1918 Mann tractor 'Myfanwy' and a 1914 Cockshutt plough at the Salop Rally in August 2002.*

OPPOSITE: *Direct ploughing demonstrated at the September 1993 Great Dorset Steam Fair, using a 7nhp 1908 Marshall traction engine named 'Margaret'.*

Chapter 6

Showman's and Heavy Haulage

THE showman's road locomotive and showman's tractor are the 'proud peacocks' of the traction-engine world. With their brightly coloured and intricately patterned paintwork, brass barley twists supporting the canopies and huge, spoked wheels painted in lined colours, and especially with their imposing bulk and size, the showman's are the best loved of all traction engines. They nearly always bore names, and even these are imposing: 'Iron Maiden', 'Supreme', 'His Majesty', 'Lady, Pride of England', 'The Gladiator', and so on. Of course, all this was done for a purpose: to excite wonder at fairs and shows. Fairground rides were nearly always painted in a similar style, some also bearing murals, and the engines became mobile advertisements for the travelling showmen and women.

Basically these engines were road locomotives with extras such as dynamos and generators. Most were bespoke and individual to the owner, and often reflected his personality. The travelling showman, moving between fairs, needed a powerful and reliable form of transport for his caravan – in itself often a work of art of mahogany and sculptured glass – and for the fairground equipment that was his livelihood. Before the coming of the steam engine, teams of horses did the work, but this was costly as horses needed feeding, care and accommodation all year

OPPOSITE: The 1914 Aveling & Porter 6nhp road locomotive 'Clyde' hauling timber at the Great Dorset Steam Fair in August 2001. It was built for S. Frampton of Farnham, Surrey, for haulage, then sold to a Fred Smith of Basingstoke in 1920 for hauling bricks. It later moved to Cornwall, and preservation, in the 1960s.

round, and men were specifically employed to look after them and drive them; and horses were slow. In the 1880s traction engines began to replace horse power, Aveling & Porter and Fowler being first in this venture. The first engines specifically prepared as showman's transports were simply traction engines modified so that a generator could be mounted and driven by the flywheel; electric lighting was a giant step forward for those days and now the canopies could be decorated with light bulbs. These engines, however simply modified, answered the need of the showmen, who could now move their caravans and attractions around the country, and when on site the engines could power and light the equipment.

Almost immediately engines were further modified by creating a platform at the front of the smokebox to carry a generator, much as we see today in preserved engines, and the showman's road locomotive had arrived. Most showman's engines in preservation have a canopy for protection of the crew, though in the first recognizable showman's engines this was not a high priority and it was not until the 1890s that they were fitted. Beautiful brass barley-twist stanchions also gradually became standard fittings, and paintwork became more and more flamboyant and customized to the showman's wishes. Another innovation, probably brought about by experience in fairgrounds, was the chimney extension to disperse smoke.

This design, once perfected, standardized the showman's engine until the First World War. The public's demand for ever more exciting rides, mirrored today by the extreme attractions offered by modern amusement parks, meant that scenic rides much bigger and requiring greater power were built to satisfy

ABOVE LEFT: The 1911 Burrell 7nhp road locomotive 'Clinker' at the Belvoir Castle Rally road run in May 2004. It was built for the Wingham Agricultural Co. in Kent for road haulage, then purchased in the 1920s by Mornement & Ray of East Harling, Middlesex and sometimes used for dredging in the Fens.

ABOVE RIGHT: The 1914 Burrell 7nhp road locomotive 'Lord Kitchener' in the Three Counties Steam Tour of May 1993 at Framlingham, Suffolk, followed by a Scammell.

The 1915 Burrell 8nhp crane engine, basically a traction engine, showing how the various types carried out the work of others – usually a crane engine would be a road locomotive. This engine is seen at the July 1999 Weeting Rally.

Charles Burrell & Sons Ltd

The celebrated traction-engine manufacturers Charles Burrell & Sons can be traced back to the second half of the eighteenth century. In 1770 Joseph Burrell opened a smithy in St Nicholas Street, Thetford, the ancient county town of East Anglia. Joseph, as well as repairing existing agricultural machinery, proceeded to produce his own farming equipment such as seeding machines. These won prizes for their workmanship, an ethic that continued throughout the firm's long life.

In the early years of the nineteenth century the smithy grew to become the St Nicholas Works, and produced many forms of agricultural equipment including ploughs, harrows, saw benches and so on. It was inevitable, therefore, that this firm should show an early interest in the steam traction engine; it was well placed with a foundry, a works and a workforce skilled in engineering.

The first Charles Burrell (two other family members born during the century were named Charles and contributed to the success of the firm) was born in 1817, grandson of the founder Joseph. He lived until 1906, through the glory years of the works, and had become Works Manager in 1836. By this time the first portables were being designed: a William Howden of Boston built the first of its type in 1839 and Burrell were not far behind because in 1846 their first portable – appropriately designated No. 1 – was produced. It must have been a sound design from the start as this portable worked for another forty years, finally being bought back by the firm in 1884 to use as a display exhibit. That same year the firm became a limited company.

Burrell collaborated with a James Boydell, who had patented a design of wheels for traction-engine use, and in 1856 a Burrell-Boydell road locomotive was built, steered by a forecarriage also using Boydell wheels. This machine, as well as being a road steam locomotive for haulage, was demonstrated for direct ploughing. These engines cost over £1,000 to buy – an enormous sum at that time, possibly over £100,000 at today's prices.

Much design work was carried out through the mid-decades of the nineteenth century and in 1860 Burrell built their first self-propelled traction engine. As with other manufacturers' engines the steersman sat at the front of the engine and operated a ship-style wheel, but by the 1870s the Burrell traction engine resembled the self-propelled direct-steered engines that we see preserved today. Other agricultural machines were also produced around this time, in particular the steam ploughing engine. Burrell were always keen to collaborate with other inventors, and in 1871 they formed an alliance with R.W. Thomson to fit his solid rubber tyres to their road locomotives.

Like most of the other firms famed for their road steam engines, Burrells diversified, but not just into farming products like their own threshing machines: a real departure came in the 1880s with steam launches, and then full-size marine engines. Steam tram engines were also designed, and two were supplied to Bradford and Birmingham tram companies. Development was not neglected on road steam and many innovations and refinements were made such as compounding (the re-use of steam in the engine), and clutch and change-speed mechanisms.

The steam road roller was added to the range in 1891, this having a compound engine and a patented scarifier to break up the road surface. Road locomotives were kitted out for the showman from the 1900s, either as full-size or the smaller showman's tractor; these were well liked by the fairground fraternity because of their superb build quality. In 1908 RAC-sponsored trials for steam tractors were entered by Burrells and the only Gold Medal awarded for all-round efficiency was won by the firm: from this the celebrated Gold Medal Tractor was born, much sought after in preservation. The final addition to the Burrell portfolio was the overtype steam wagon, the first rolling off the production line in 1911.

Burrell exported engines to other countries, especially the 'Colonial' type. Some were designed to burn straw, for places where coal or wood was not available such as the prairies of South America. The 1920s saw the contraction of markets and Burrell were one of the firms joining a consortium called Agriculture and General Engines Ltd of 1919. This company only existed for ten years or so and collapsed in 1932, marking the end of this illustrious firm. The last Burrell engine built – by Garretts of Leiston on licence – was no. 4094, a traction engine, and is preserved.

In the firm's lifetime Burrells were sought after because of their superb build quality and legendary reliability. This still holds true in preservation, some 330 of all types being preserved in Great Britain and others abroad.

The 1919 Burrell 5nhp road locomotive 'Winifred' being prepared for a road run based around Stroud in May 2004.

ABOVE: The unique 1912 Brown & May 6nhp showman's road locomotive 'General Buller' next to a set of gallopers at the Weeting Rally in 1993.

TOP LEFT: The 1931 Burrell 5nhp road locomotive 'Dorothy' pictured at the Quainton Road Railway Centre in June 2001, posed in the station forecourt. This engine was the last but one Burrell to be built, in 1931, and was built by Garretts of Leiston. It worked for C. Singleton, a contractor from Rackenford, Devon, and in Gloucestershire. At one time it was owned by the famous Arthur Napper of Appleford.

LEFT: The 1913 Foden road locomotive 'Monarch' at the Royal Hospital School, Holbrook in May 1999, preparing for the Great Eastern road run.

ABOVE LEFT: *The 1917 8nhp Fowler road locomotive 'Kingfisher' at the Quainton Road Railway Centre in June 2001, posed on the station forecourt.*

ABOVE RIGHT: *The 1919 10nhp McLaren road locomotive 'Boadicea' at the Great Dorset Steam Fair heavy-haulage display in September 1999. Sold to the War Office to pull heavy guns, though never exported, she worked in heavy haulage for a time before being rebuilt as a showman's engine by Edward Corrigan of Filey, Yorkshire and called 'Gigantic'. She was reincarnated as a road locomotive and worked in haulage for Shaw & Gaskell of Hull, and later in life also undertook fen drainage until laid up in 1958.*

RIGHT: *The 1928 8nhp Fowler road locomotive 'Atlas' seen with a haulage load, a transformer, at Castlemorton Common, near Malvern in July 2001. 'Atlas' was one of the last road engines to enter service with haulage contactor Norman Box before the business was sold to Pickfords; it worked out of Manchester until 1948.*

The 1913 6nhp Burrell showman's road locomotive 'King George VI' stands next to gallopers at the Gloucestershire Warwickshire Railway Steam Rally at Toddington in October 2002. This engine was sold new to Swales Bolesworth, a London showman, being sold to E. Andrews Jnr of Tunbridge Wells three years later. She worked up to Second World War, and was later purchased for preservation.

BELOW LEFT: The 1921 5nhp Burrell traction engine 'St Brannock' at the Welland Rally in July 2000. This picture demonstrates that the line between engines is blurred: traction engines were used for haulage like road locomotives, and this traction engine carries showman's fittings.

CENTRE: The 1915 5nhp Burrell showman's road locomotive 'Nero' on a road run in Bedfordshire in May 2004, near Gamlingay, with a showman's caravan attached.

RIGHT: The 1921 8nhp Burrell showman's road locomotive 'Lord Lascelles' at the Astle Park Rally in an evocative fairground location, in August 1994.

William Foster & Co. Ltd

This firm started life in 1856 at Wellington Foundry, Lincoln. William Foster (1816–76), was actually a miller, and the foundry at first turned out grinding-mill equipment and various agricultural machinery. The firm was called William Foster, Engineer, at first, but it became a limited liability company in 1877 called William Foster & Co. Ltd.

The use of machinery in agriculture was taking off, and Foster built his first portable steam engine in 1858. Both horizontal- and vertical-boiler portables were built and various adaptations such as winding engines were made. Eventually the wide range and types meant that other stationary boilers such as locomotive, Cornish- or Lancashire-style could be made and supplied. The 1860s saw expansion of this side of the business as Foster portables became very popular at home and abroad.

Partly because of the success of their portable range and agricultural machinery, Fosters did not build a self-moving traction engine until 1889; from then on sizes from 4–8nhp were produced. Fosters were also well known for their agricultural machinery, and in particular produced a threshing machine for use with their traction engines. Once they had started building road steam, Fosters built some very fine road locomotives of 7 and 8nhp from 1903, many of which were used as showman's engines. In all sixty-eight were built in the period up to 1934, the firm becoming the third largest producer of showman's road locomotives after Burrell and Fowlers. Fosters also entered the steam-tractor market in response to the Heavy Motor Car Orders 1904, which cleared the way for this type of road steam for light haulage. The 5-ton tractor was called a 'Wellington Tractor'; it had a compound engine and rear-axle springing, and proved very popular. It is interesting that Fosters were one of the very few of the major steam engineering firms that never produced a steam road roller.

An interesting joint effort between Fosters and Richard Hornsby & Sons Ltd was the Foster-Hornsby Chain Track Haulage Engine of 1910. The main engine and transmission was made by Fosters and the chain tracks by Hornsby. This was a traction engine on chain-driven tracks, for use on difficult terrain, but though it was tested thoroughly nothing came of this unique machine. Amazingly, part of this engine survives, preserved on Vancouver Island, Canada.

Fosters was one of the first manufacturers to recognize the need to export their products, and early on established a branch works in Budapest, and later on produced specialist engines for the South American market, including internal combustion-engined tractors in 1911.

The First World War saw Fosters do a great deal of development work on tanks, which they also built, and because of this after the conflict all road steam engines produced show a small replica of a tank as part of the trade mark.

The last road steam built by Fosters was the overtype steam wagon, sixty of which were produced between 1919 and 1933, of which one has been preserved. Fosters saw that steam power could not last and from the 1930s concentrated on other engineering products, though still having a hand in the market – in fact, portables were still being made by the firm in the 1940s and Fosters are reputed to have made the very last traction engine built in this country, which was delivered in 1942.

There are sixty-eight Foster steam engines in preservation, including seven of their beautifully crafted showman's road locomotives.

This 1916 7nhp Foster showman's road locomotive, 'Admiral Beatty', is seen in the fairground at the August 2001 Great Dorset Steam Fair. Not initially built as a showman's, she was converted by Foster in the 1920s to full specification and worked for Thurston & Sons, hauling rides.

A splendid line-up of showman's road locomotive and tractors at the St Agnes Rally in August 1992.

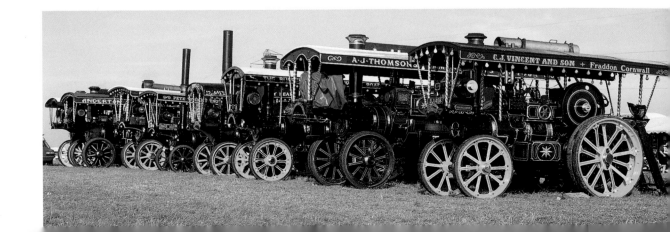

The 1916 10nhp Fowler showman's road locomotive 'Valiant' is seen next to a fairground organ at the Bedfordshire Rally in September 2003.

ABOVE: This 1924 Burrell 10nhp showman's road locomotive 'Ex-Mayor' was at the Bedfordshire Rally in September 2003. This engine was built new for the famous fairground operators G.T. Tuby & Sons of Doncaster, and named after one of the civic positions held by the firm's founder.

BELOW RIGHT: A 4nhp Foster showman's tractor, 'John Michael' dates from 1939 and was the last one built by this firm. She is seen here at the Belvoir Castle Rally, Leicestershire in May 2004.

This 1920 6nhp Clayton & Shuttleworth showman's road locomotive, 'Old England', is one of only two of this type preserved. It is seen here in the fairground at the Welland Rally in July 2000.

The 1917 class 4CD 4nhp Garrett tractor 'Countess', with showman's fittings, is seen here with living caravan at the July 1992 Rushmoor Rally.

The 1915 10nhp Fowler showman's road locomotive 'Carry-On' in the fairground at the Rushmoor Rally in July 1992. This engine, like many, was commandeered by the War Office to haul guns. Afterwards she was converted to full showman's specification by Charles Openshaw of Reading in 1923 and worked for Codonas in Scotland. Sold in 1943 to McGivens in Northern Ireland, she was last used in 1958 before preservation.

BELOW: The 1932 10nhp Fowler showman's road locomotive 'Lion', appropriately of the famed 'Super Lion' class, was surely the pinnacle and mighty last flowering of road steam, though only four were built. This engine is seen at Stanway Hall in Gloucestershire in October 2003. The engine was built for the famous Anderton & Rowlands of Bristol and worked the fairgrounds until laid up in 1946, and was then preserved in the 1950s.

ABOVE: The 1920 7nhp Fowler showman's road locomotive 'Iron Maiden/Kitchener' at the Belvoir Castle Rally, Leicestershire in May 2004. 'Iron Maiden' is famous for her starring role in the 1960s film of the same name. She started life as the road locomotive 'Kitchener' for F. Barnes Ltd of Portland, Dorset. Rebuilt to full showman's specification by Fowlers, she worked for Mrs H. Oadley of Alfreton, Derbyshire on the fairgrounds, before preservation in the 1950s.

Brief Histories of other Steam Builders

There were many and varied builders of road steam engines in Great Britain: some of them giants of industry; some producing just a handful; some specializing in one type only; and some flourishing for a while before closing down. In many cases no examples of their work exist, only the memory lingers on. The following are a few of those firms.

Wm. Allchin Ltd This was a small, local concern at Globe Works, Northampton, with less than 100 employees, yet producing some well-built steam engines, of which twenty-one are preserved. The works started in 1847, building agricultural machinery, portables and, from 1872, traction engines, of which in the end 220 were built. The works also built fourteen steam road rollers, six road locomotives and one showman's engine, but overtype steam wagons totalled 256 and seven undertypes were also built. The works closed in 1931.

Sir W.G. Armstrong-Whitworth Ltd This giant general engineering firm built a number of steam road rollers as a one-off exercise in the 1920s, of which seven are preserved.

Barrows & Stewart These were built at Banbury, Oxfordshire and were all portables, of which three from the 1870s are preserved.

Brown & May Ltd A well-known firm in its day, whose works were at Devizes, Wiltshire. Brown & May was famed for its portables, of which twelve are preserved; also preserved are one tractor and a showman's road locomotive from 1912, called 'General Buller'.

Davey, Paxman & Co. Ltd This was a prolific general engineering firm from Colchester, Essex. All types of engines were built from 1865, and in 1940 the firm amalgamated with Ruston & Hornsby Ltd. Sixteen engines are preserved: eleven portables and five traction engines.

Alfred Dodman & Co. Ltd Alfred Dodman was born in 1832 at Tichwell, Norfolk, and founded the Highgate Works at King's Lynn in 1854. Portables were built at first, then traction engines from 1872. The firm was particularly noted for its stationary engines of all types, including hoist engines and marine engines. Dodman also built a few railway locomotives. In 1931 Dodman purchased E.S. Hindley & Co. and concentrated on oil engines. None are preserved.

C.J. Fowell Ltd This was a low-volume producer of road steam engines based at Cromwell Iron Works, St Ives, Huntingdonshire. Seven are preserved, all of them traction engines from 1902–22.

T. Green & Sons Ltd Green built steam road rollers from the 1890s to the late 1920s at the Smithfield Iron Works, Leeds. Five of these rollers are preserved.

J. & F. Howard Howard built traction engines, ploughing engine and agricultural equipment at Britannia Iron Works, Bedford. One traction engine and one ploughing engine are preserved from the 1860s–70s.

Mann Patent Steam Cart & Wagon Co. Ltd Based at Hunslet, Leeds, close to the Fowler and McLaren factories, this firm is best known for its wagons, of undertype and overtype design, which were built from 1903; tractors and road rollers were also built. The steam tractor was advertised at the time as being purpose built for direct ploughing, but was not particularly successful. Eight of these are preserved, along with four wagons and one road roller.

Merryweather & Shand-Mason Ltd Both these London-based firms concentrated on building steam fire and pump engines from the 1860s to the 1940s; these were basically portables, because in use they would be pulled by teams of horses. Their products were bought not just by local authorities, but also by private estates and large commercial concerns. Seventy Merryweathers have been preserved, and fifty Shand-Masons, often by the Fire Authorities for which they once worked.

Savage Bros Ltd A well-known firm at St Nicholas Iron Works, Kings Lynn, Norfolk, Savage built traction engines, one of which from 1889 is preserved. However, the firm is best known for its centre engines in fairground rides and organ engines; it also built steam yacht and lighting engines. Two full-size replica traction engines were built by Belmec Intl to Savage Bros designs. Over ninety of the engines have been preserved.

W. Tasker & Sons Ltd Tasker's were blacksmith and implement makers at Waterloo Iron Works, Andover, Hampshire. Their first traction engine was built in 1869; they also built portables, road rollers and, in the 1920s, overtype wagons, and are best known for their 'Little Giant' steam tractors. Tasker was never a large producer of steam engines, and was often in financial difficulties. Nevertheless, thirty-eight have been preserved of most types, including one wagon kept at the Milestones Museum, Basingstoke.

Robert Tidman & Sons At their Bishops Bridge Iron Works, Norwich, Tidman mostly built portables but are also known for their centre and organ engines. Twenty-two are preserved, including two portables.

Wm Tuxford & Sons Founded by William Tuxford, agricultural engineers, the works was at Boston and Skirbeck Iron Works, Boston. Their first portable was built in 1850; this was followed by traction engines, some with the Boydell principle (like Burrells), from the 1860s. Tuxford also built stationary engines and beam engines, but the works closed in 1887. Eight portables are preserved, all from the 1880s.

Wantage Engineering Co. Ltd Based in Wantage Berkshire (now Oxfordshire), this firm built portables, traction engines and, from 1903, undertype wagons. Two traction engines are preserved, from 1900 and 1908.

STEAM WAGONS

There were a surprising number of steam-wagon-only manufacturers from the 1890s onwards, though only a few stayed the course. Some of the better-known firms not already illustrated are as follows:

Atkinson & Co. Undertype wagons built at Frenchwood Works, Preston, Lancashire. One wagon from 1918 is preserved, imported from Australia.

Lancashire Steam Wagon Company Building mostly undertypes from 1906, this firm became Leyland Motors. Two preserved.

John I. Thornycroft & Co. Ltd Built from 1899 at Basingstoke, Hampshire. Three preserved, including a van.

Yorkshire Patent Steam Wagon Co. Built undertype wagons at Hunslet, Leeds from 1904 to 1929. Seven preserved.

Other builders of which none are preserved:
Bristol Wagon & Carriage Works, Lawrence Hill, Bristol.
T. Coulthard & Sons Ltd, Cooper Road, Preston, Lancashire.
Jesse Ellis & Co. Ltd, Invicta Works, Maidstone, Kent.
Naylor & Co., Hereford.
St Pancras Ironworks Co. Ltd, Holloway, North London.
Standard Steam Lorry & Omnibus Co., Rayleigh, Essex.
Straker Steam Vehicle Co. Ltd, Bristol.

Chapter 7
Preservation

THERE is something undeniably fascinating about steam, which turns grown-ups into youngsters, whether it be railway, road and agricultural steam, or just the nostalgia that surrounds it. Why do normally sane people spend money and many hours working on steam engines, often in inclement conditions, or chasing across the country just to see them in action? The reasons have been explored over and over again, but I suppose it is partly simple nostalgia for the bygone times represented by steam, and for the elemental force that inhabits these engines once the fire turns water into steam.

Steam engines can be beautiful artefacts in their own right, with gleaming brass and paintwork, and shapes that please the eye. To this is added the wonderful smell of coal, hot oil and steam and, of course, the human element, the crew, without whose involvement these machines would not move. Enthusiasm for steam, once it bites, takes no prisoners: the hackneyed phrase 'from dustmen to princes' is a truism but the steam movement is a classless society.

Preservation

There are two main organizations that look after the interests of the road-steam enthusiast: the Road Locomotive Society and the National Traction Engine Trust. As well as these are the many and varied traction engine clubs and the specialist and one-make associations like the Road Roller Association, the Steam Plough

Club, the Steam Car Club of Great Britain and the Sentinel Drivers Club – the list is endless. There is also the specialist press that covers events and the history of the movement, magazines like *Old Glory*, *Vintage Spirit*, and *World's Fair*, and also the many club and society house publications.

The Road Locomotive Society was set up in 1937 by like-minded enthusiasts to encourage restoration and to document the history of road steam, which it still does admirably to this day. The National Traction Engine Trust was founded in 1954 by seven engine owners who set up the Traction Engine Owners Club; ordinary members were admitted in 1957 and the club, which became a trust in 1985, now has some 3,500 members. Its aim is to look after all aspects of the traction-engine movement, and it publishes an excellent and informative quarterly magazine, *Steaming*. The Trust celebrated its fiftieth year with a display of rarely seen engines at the 2004 Great Dorset Steam Fair and a very successful anniversary road run in Northamptonshire in September 2004.

There are traction-engine and vintage-machinery clubs all over the country, usually regionally based, with enthusiastic members who meet regularly and in a lot of cases organize a road run or local steam rally, and who are the backbone of the movement. Similar to the clubs are the one-make or specialist associations, like the Road Roller Association and the Sentinel Drivers Club, working with the national bodies and the rally organizers to promote their own particular interest.

Another important area that brings the movement to the general public is the museums specializing in traction engines, some general, some one-make. The Charles Burrell Museum at Thetford and the Long Shop at Leiston are one-makes (the latter for Garretts), and rail and road steam examples include Bressingham Steam and the Hollycombe Steam Collection; there are many more around Great Britain. There are also, of course, many other museums that have a corner where road steam is highlighted.

OPPOSITE: The 'Super Lion' class 10nhp 'Supreme' was the final showman's engine built by Fowlers, in 1934. She is seen here on a road run by the roadside near Adderbury on her way to Bloxham and the Banbury Rally in 2004. Sold to Mrs Deakin of Brynmawr, South Wales, with specialized fitments such as the chromed barley-twist canopy struts for fairground work, she was commandeered to haul railway locomotives in Glasgow in the Second World War and finally entered preservation in 1958.

The Carters Famous Travelling Steam Fair is a living museum; as the name suggests it is a traditional funfair with steam-driven gallopers, yachts, dodgems, chairoplanes and other traditional fairground equipment. This fair travels to various venues throughout the Thames Valley and London from March to October and recreates the glory days of the traditional steam fair.

We now come to the enthusiasts who started the movement and still carry it forward, the hands-on preservationists and engine owners, and their crews. Back in the 1950s, road steam engines were often rescued for small sums from scrapyards or worse, or even – like some road rollers – bought out of service. It is unlikely that these early enthusiasts could have foreseen the position fifty years later, when nostalgia for steam continues to grow and has turned into a leisure industry giving pleasure to many thousands, and engines change hands for huge sums.

Working road steam, apart from a few isolated areas, virtually died out in the middle years of the twentieth century. Almost immediately the preservation era began, nurtured through the 1950s and really taking off in the 1960s. Vehicle preservation was not a new hobby: veteran cars had been collected and renovated for some time, as had ancient motorcycles. In those early days steam vehicles were cheap to buy, even if running them was a different matter. In the 1950s there were a large number of out of service or derelict engines lying in yards all over the country, often where they had finished work. Some, like steam road rollers or wagons, could be bought out of service from local authorities or contractors. Some traction engines were kept as 'pets' by their owners, and some farmers and contractors kept their steam engines because of their conservative views and maybe as a protest against 'newfangled ideas'. These engines were perfect for the enthusiast as most did not require extensive repair and could be used immediately.

Steam 'parties' or 'meets', the forerunners of the steam rally, took off in the 1950s, originally just for club members to bring along and show off their acquisitions, but eventually the public were admitted and extra cash became available to enhance the meetings, and rallies were born.

There are many differences between the situation today and the fledgling movement in the 1950s, not least in the prices paid for engines. In the 1950s they changed hands for very modest sums, often scrap value, and the Traction Engine Club once even raffled an engine! Today these engines are treated as antiques and the prices reflect that, five-figure sums being paid for even the humble road roller, and a road locomotive possibly commanding a six-figure price.

The commercial value of an engine makes it difficult for younger or first-time club members to get started with their own engine. One compensation is that steam engines are labour intensive and crews are always required, so that is one way of being involved. The National Traction Engine Trust has for some time sponsored the Steam Apprentices Club, where the young and not-so-young enthusiast can learn how to maintain and drive a steam engine; this scheme has already born fruit and will pay dividends in the future.

Another important aspect of preservation is safety. All boilers have to be examined by a qualified inspector on an annual basis to obtain insurance. Repairs to boilers are usually carried out by professionals, of which there are now several, thanks to the road and rail steam preservation movement.

Some owners attempt most restoration work themselves, apart from specialist areas like boilers, while others will entrust the majority of the work to professional restorers. There is no question that actually buying a traction engine is only the start: maintenance costs are high, as are overheads like coal, oil, insurance, rally transport and so on. One saving grace of the cost of purchase and repair and maintenance is that the annual turnover of engines on the rally field is consequently high, and actively encourages interest for the enthusiast and the paying public.

It is fairly safe to say that the supply of derelict engines has dried up in the United Kingdom, though it is possible that in a barn somewhere lives an undiscovered engine. However, for an enthusiast wishing to purchase an engine requiring complete or partial restoration the only recourse is to attempt to import from abroad. These supplies are running out as well and in some countries, notably in the Antipodes, government restrictions are being placed on the export of their heritage.

There does not seem to be a shortage of newcomers to the movement, possibly because of the challenge afforded by the maintenance and driving of a steam engine in today's sanitized world. When these engines are driven on the road the experience is quite alien to those used to being cosseted in modern transport, with so many things that require constant attention. The correct gear for the road, the effort of operating chain steering, the state of fire and water, and coal supplies – not to mention the ever more crowded highways, traffic lights, roundabouts and speed bumps – all these and more need careful consideration from the crew of a traction engine.

It is to be hoped that road steam will continue for many years to come, both at rallies and on the road, but legislation and health and safety regulations become ever more pervasive. It would be a sad day indeed if live steam were to be banished, and only museums were to benefit from static exhibits of our once-proud heritage.

Steam Rallies

Steam rallies play an important part in the preservation of traction engines. Owners and their crews can show off their pride and joy, meet fellow owners, operate them at working sites, or enjoy roading to and from the rally. Enthusiasts can enjoy the sight and sound of steam, take photographs and talk to the owners. The general public can also enjoy and learn about these living antiques of steam in action at close quarters, and everybody can take in the other attractions that are part of the scene at rallies: the stalls, the other vintage and classic machinery, and the company of like-minded people.

The current rally scene is very different from the tentative beginnings some fifty years ago, but then the austere 1950s are a world away from the sophisticated consumer society of the first decade of the 21st century. In the early 1950s it must be remembered that some road steam still worked for real: some threshing, ploughing or dredging was done by steam at farms eager to keep to the old ways, showman's locomotives were in use at some fairs, steam wagons – usually Sentinel or Fodens – could be seen on the roads, and road rollers would remain in use for another decade or so. Therefore, enthusiasm for the commonplace or recently discarded may have appeared bizarre to some.

It was therefore a different type of person who attended the early rallies: they were basically club members enjoying themselves at their annual outing, and if others wished to come along, then all well and good. While an old traction engine or road roller, possibly just out of service or languishing in a scrapyard, could be had for a reasonable sum in those days, money was tight so soon after the Second World War and austerity measures only just finished. Money was probably not available for something that was seen by many as merely scrap metal, or indeed to spend on a visit to a local meeting of enthusiasts.

The famous 'Wager for Ale' in 1950, between Arthur Napper and his 1902 Marshall traction engine 'Old Timer' and Miles Chetwynd-Stapylton DFC and his 1918 Aveling & Porter traction engine 'Ladygrove', changed matters. These races were extensively reported and raised the profile of road-steam preservation, and the club meetings and rallies benefited from the attendance of members of the public. Even so, the steam rally as we know it today did not take off until the 1960s: quite a few of the current rallies are only just celebrating forty years of existence and many others are decades less old. The greatest rally of them all, the Great Dorset Steam Fair, reached its thirty-sixth meeting in 2004.

The rallygoer is spoilt for choice today. Every weekend from May to September a number of rallies are held in various parts of the country. Size and content is variable, from small village fairs with a couple of steamers in attendance, which attract just a few hundred, to the three- or four-day event where up to a hundred steam engines may be seen, with all the other attractions necessary to keep the rallygoer and his family occupied, and many thousands of visitors. Most of these rallies are still run by traction engine clubs, though a few of the larger rallies, including the Great Dorset, are run as businesses.

The Great Dorset Steam Fair, which began in 1969, is the largest rally of its kind in the world. Held over five days at the end of August and early September, it attracts crowds of up to a quarter of a million. The site is currently on rolling chalk farmlands at Tarrant Hinton in Dorset. The Fair is the creation of Michael Oliver MBE, who from humble beginnings in 1969, with many ups and downs, developed the Fair into arguably the greatest vintage machinery show on earth. His son Martin has now taken charge of operations.

The amount of vintage and classic machinery that forms the exhibits is truly awe-inspiring: in 2004 nearly 400 steam engines attended, along with diesel tractors, classic cars, commercial vehicles, motorcycles, stationary engines, fairground organs and so on. The working demonstrations are held all over the site, ploughing, threshing, saw benches, road making and the fairground all competing for attention.

The fairground theme boasts the largest gathering of showman's road locomotives anywhere (over sixty in 2004), and to see the impressive line-up next to the working fairground and the evening with the engines lit up is magical. A must is the so-called 'playpen' where steam and some heavy commercials test out their machines, often with heavy haulage loads on the steep hill at the far end of the site. All day long the spectacle continues, sometimes clouded with dust from the chalk, but always exciting and entertaining. To many enthusiasts it is an annual pilgrimage, indeed a national institution, not to be missed at any cost: anybody who cares about our national heritage and its preservation should attend once in their life.

Rallies are often advertised locally or information can be gained from the periodicals catering for steam enthusiasts such as *Old Glory*, *Vintage Spirit* and *World's Fair*, all of which list the year's rallies; alternatively, the National Traction Engine Trust approves a number of rallies during the year and issues a listing to members and interested parties.

LEFT: The 1920 8nhp Fowler showman's road locomotive 'Repulse' is seen next to a fairground ride at the former Stratford upon Avon Shire Horse Centre in 1995.

BELOW LEFT: The fate of a few redundant steam road rollers was to become a children's plaything in a public park. Here, one such Aveling & Porter road roller resides in Victoria Park, Leamington Spa in October 1992. This roller has since been sold into preservation.

BELOW RIGHT: The 1937 7nhp Foster traction engine 'Saint' at the Old Warden Rally in September 2004.

ABOVE: The only Fodens showman's road locomotive preserved, this 1910-built 8nhp model is called 'Prospector/Jane' and is seen at the July 1993 Pickering Rally, North Yorkshire.

This 6nhp Aveling & Porter tractor, named 'Nippy', built in 1926, is seen outside the Royal Hospital School, Holbrook, Suffolk, at the Eastern Counties road run in May 1999.

ABOVE: *The 1920 7nhp Fowler road locomotive 'Sir Douglas' taking part in the Great Eastern road run in April 1998, in rural Suffolk.*

LEFT: *The 1908 6nhp Garrett showman's road locomotive 'British Hero' is pictured here in the fairground at the June 2002 Banbury Rally. She was built new for Alfred Dawson of Rushmere St Andrew, Norfolk for haulage duties, sold to Sheppards in 1911 and then converted to full showman's specification. In 1935 was purchased by John Rendle of New Bolingbroke, Lincolnshire and then went into preservation in the mid-1950s.*

Major Road Steam Museums and Societies

Barleylands Craft Village & Farm Centre
Barleylands Road
Billericay
Essex
Tel: 01268 290229

Bicton Park & Countryside Museum
East Budleigh Salterton
Devon

Bolton Steam Museum (mill engines)
Mornington Road
Off Chorley Old Road
Bolton
Lancashire
Tel. 01257 265003

Bradford Industrial Museum
(stationary steam)
Moorside Mills
Moorside Road
Bradford
West Yorkshire
Tel: 01274 435900

Breamore Countryside Museum
Breamore House
Fordingbridge
Hampshire
Tel: 01725 512468

Bressingham Steam Museum
Bressingham
Diss
Norfolk
Tel: 01379 687386

British Commercial Vehicle Museum
King Street
Leyland
Preston
Lancashire
Tel: 01772 451011

The Charles Burrell Museum
Minstergate
Thetford
Norfolk

Bygones Museum
Claydon
Banbury
Oxfordshire
Tel: 01295 690258

Carters Famous Travelling Steam Fair
Tel: 01628 822221

Coors Visitor Centre (formerly Bass)
Horninglow Street
Burton-upon-Trent
Staffs
Tel: 0845 6000598

Dingles Steam Museum
Milford
Lifton
Devon
Tel: 01566 783425

Hollycombe Steam Collection
Iron Hill
Liphook
Hampshire
Tel: 01428 724900

Kew Bridge Steam Museum
Green Dragon Lane
Brentford
Middlesex
Tel: 020 8568 4757

Klondyke Mill Preservation Centre
Draycott in the Clay
Sudbury
Staffordshire
Tel: 01283 820806

Long Shop Museum (Garretts)
Main Street
Leiston
Suffolk
Tel: 01728 832189

Markham Grange Steam Museum
(stationary steam)
Longlands Lane
Brodsworth
Doncaster
South Yorkshire
Tel: 01302 330430

Milestones
Hampshire Living History Museum
Leisure Park
Basingstoke
Tel: 01962 846315

Museum of East Anglian Life
Stowmarket
Suffolk
Tel: 01449 612229

Museum of English Rural Life
University of Reading
Redlands Road
Reading
Tel: 0118 3788660

Norfolk Rural Life Museum
Beach House
Gressenhall
Dereham
Norfolk
Tel: 01362 860563

Strumpshaw Hall Steam Museum
Strumpshaw
Norwich
Norfolk
Tel: 01603 713392

Tinkers Park Collection
Hadlow Down
Uckfield
Sussex

World of Country Life
Sandy Bay
Exmouth
Devon
Tel: 01395 274533

SOCIETIES
National Traction Engine Trust
Membership Secretary:
Mr J.R. Cook
'Dolfarni'
74 Church Lane
Kirkby la Thorpe
Sleaford
Lincolnshire
NG34 9NU
Tel: 01529 303160

National Vintage Tractor and Engine Club
Membership Secretary:
Mrs P.E. Sims
1 Hall Farm Cottages
Church Lane
Swarkestone
Derby
DE73 1JB

Road Roller Association
Membership Secretary:
Mrs D. Rayner
'Invicta'
9 Beagle Ridge Drive
Acomb
York
YO24 3JH
Tel: 01904 331926

Steam Plough Club
Membership Secretary:
Mr Sean Symons
1 Westcott Cottage
Moretonhampstead
Newton Abbot
Devon
Tel: 01647 441147

Bibliography

Bell, B., *Ransomes, Sims & Jefferies* (Old Pond Publishing, 2001)

Clark, R.H., *Steam Engine Builders of Lincolnshire* (SLHA, 1998)

Clark, R.H., *Steam Engine Builders of Norfolk* (Haynes Publishing, 1988)

Crawley, J., *Ploughing Engines in Focus* (John Crawley Publishing, 1985)

Crawley, J., *Steam Rollers in Focus* (John Crawley Publishing, 1986)

Crawley, J., *Steam Traction Engines in Camera* (John Crawley Publishing, 1987)

Crawley, J., *Steam Wagons in Focus* (John Crawley Publishing, 1984)

Hughes, W. and Thomas, A. & J., *The Sentinel*, Volumes 1 & 2 (David & Charles, 1973)

Lane, M.R., *The Story of St Nicholas Works* (Unicorn Press, 1994)

Lane, M.R., *The Story of the Britannia Iron Works* (Quiller Press, London, 1993)

Lane, M.R., *The Story of the Steam Plough Works* (Northgate Publishing, 1980)

Lane, M.R., *The Story of the Wellington Foundry, Lincoln* (Unicorn Press, London, 1997)

Middlemiss, J.L. and Sawford, E., *Wm Allchin Ltd, Northampton* (Alan T. Condie Publishing, 1990)

Mortons Heritage Media, *Old Glory* magazine, editor: Colin Tyson

NTET, *Steaming* (NTET house magazine, editor: Roger West)

Pease, John, *The History of J. & H. McLaren of Leeds* (Landmark Publishing, 2003)

Preston, J.M., *Aveling & Porter* (North Kent Books, 1987)

Rayner, D.A., *Road Rollers*, Shire Album no. 281, (Shire Publications, 1992)

Rayner, D.A., *Steam Wagons* (Shire Publications, 2003)

Rayner, D.A., *Traction Engines* (Shire Publications, 2002)

Rolt, L.T.C., *Waterloo Iron Works* (David & Charles, 1969)

SCHV Preservation Trust, *The Traction Engine Register, 2004* (SCHV Preservation Trust, 2004)

Science Museum, *Companion to British Road Haulage History* (Science Museum, 2003)

Thomas, A. & J., *An Album of Sentinel Works Photographs* (Woodpecker Publications, 1992)

Toy, J.B. and Rayner, D.A., *The European Traction Engine Register* (NTET Publishing, 1995)

Various authors, *Steam Heritage Guide, 2004* (Tee Publishing, 2004)

Wansborough, W.D., *The Portable Steam Engine* (Tee Publishing, reprint 1994)

Whitehead, R.A., *Age of the Traction Engine* (Fraser, Stewart Books, reprint 1994)

Whitehead, R.A., *Garretts of Leiston* (Percival Marshall, 1964)

Whitehead, R.A., *Steam in the Village* (David & Charles, 1977)